Exercises to Accompany

THE
ESSENTIALS
OF ENGLISH

A WRITER'S HANDBOOK

Exercises to Accompany

THE ESSENTIALS OF ENGLISH

A WRITER'S HANDBOOK

Lida Baker

Exercises to Accompany
The Essentials of English: A Writer's Handbook

Copyright © 2003 by Pearson Education, Inc.
All rights reserved.
No part of this publication may be reproduced,
stored in a retrieval system, or transmitted
in any form or by any means, electronic, mechanical,
photocopying, recording, or otherwise,
without the prior permission of the publisher.

Instructors who have adopted *The Essentials of English:
A Writer's Handbook* as a textbook for a course are
authorized to duplicate portions of this workbook for
their students.

Pearson Education, 10 Bank Street, White Plains, NY 10601

Senior acquisitions editor: Laura Le Dréan
Director of development: Penny Laporte
Development editors: Karen Davy, Dana Klinek
Vice president, director of design and
    production: Rhea Banker
Executive managing editor: Linda Moser
Production manager: Ray Keating
Production editor: Lynn Contrucci
Director of manufacturing: Patrice Fraccio
Senior manufacturing buyer: Dave Dickey
Cover design: Elizabeth Carlson
Cover photo: Don Bonsey/Getty Images
Text design and composition: TSI Graphics
Text font: 10.5/12 Minion
Photo credit: page 13, Dorling Kindersley

ISBN 0-13-183037-6

LONGMAN ON THE **WEB**

Longman.com offers online resources for
teachers and students. Access our Companion
Websites, our online catalog, and our local
offices around the world.

Visit us at **longman.com**.

Printed in the United States of America
5 6 7 8 9 10—PBP—08 07

CONTENTS

The Essentials of English: A Writer's Handbook has eight main parts — The Basics, Clear Sentences, Grammar, Punctuation, Mechanics, Writing and Revising, Formats, and Reference Lists. *Exercises to Accompany The Essentials of English: A Writer's Handbook* supplements all the practice sections in the Handbook (it does not contain exercises for those sections that have no practice), and the answers to the exercises appear in the back. All the pages are perforated for easy removal.

PART 1   The Basics

1a	Nouns	1
1b	Pronouns	3
1c	Verbs	5
1d	Adjectives	6
1e	Articles	7
1f	Adverbs	8
1g	Prepositions	9
1h	Conjunctions	10
3b	Dependent clauses	11
4a	Sentence parts	13

PART 2   Clear Sentences

6a	Making compound sentences	14
6b	Connecting words with coordinating conjunctions	16
6c	Connecting words with correlative conjunctions	17
6d	Using parallel forms	19
7a	Making complex sentences	20
7b	Using appositives	24
7d	Using shortened adverb clauses	26
8a	Fragments	27
8b	Run-together sentences	28
8c	Choppy writing	29
8d	Overuse of *and, but,* and *so*	30
9b	Inverted (verb-subject) word order	32
9c	Word order of direct and indirect objects	34
9d	Varying sentence openings	36
10b–c	Informal language and slang/Gender-sensitive (sexist) language	37

PART 3　Grammar

11b	Verb tenses	39
11c	Special tense combinations	47
11d	Modals	56
11e	Passive voice	60
12a	Gerunds	63
12b	Infinitives	69
12c	Gerunds vs. infinitives	77
12d	Phrasal verbs	79
13	Subject-Verb Agreement	81
14a–c	Nouns: Count and noncount	82
14d	Expressing quantity	84
15a	Articles for generic nouns: *a, an,* or no article (Ø)	85
15c	Articles for definite nouns: *the*	86
15	Articles	87
16a–b	Subject, object, and possessive pronouns/Special situations	89
16c–d	*Myself, ourselves/Each other* and *one another*	91
17	Pronoun Agreement	92
18	Pronouns: Unclear Reference	93
19	Adjectives and Adverbs: Position	94
20b	Order of adjectives	95
20c	Participial adjectives: *boring* or *bored?*	96
21	Comparisons	98
22	Negatives	100
23	Adjective Clauses	101

PART 4　Punctuation

24	End Punctuation	103
25a	Commas in compound sentences	104
25b	Commas after introducers	105
25c	Commas around extra-information modifiers	106
25d	Commas with transition signals	108
25e–f	Commas with direct quotations/Commas with items in a series	109
25g	Other uses of commas	110
26	Semicolons	111
27	Colons	112
28a	Apostrophes with possessives	113
28	Apostrophes	114
29	Quotation Marks	115
30–31	Parentheses/Dashes	116

PART 5 **Mechanics**

33	Capital Letters	117
34	Hyphens	119
35	Underlining and Italics	120
36	Abbreviations	121
37	Numbers	122
38a–c	Spelling	123

PART 6 **Writing and Revising**

40b	Organizing	125
40	The Writing Process	127
41a	Topic sentence	129
41b	Supporting sentences	130
41c	Paragraph unity	131
41d	Paragraph coherence	132
41e	Concluding sentence	134
42a	Introduction	135
42c	Conclusion	136
	Answer Key	137

1a   Nouns

PRACTICE I

Find the nouns in the following sentences. Underline the twenty-two common nouns. Circle the nine proper nouns. (*For help, see page 2 of the Handbook.*)

EXAMPLE

(George Washington) was the first <u>president</u> of the (United States.)

1. In 2002, the Olympics were held in Salt Lake City, Utah.

2. The opening ceremonies were on February 8, 2002.

3. The Olympic flame arrived in the United States on a plane from Athens, Greece.

4. The flame was carried across the country on foot, by plane, by train, by ship, by dogsled, and by snowmobile.

5. The Winter Olympic events included figure skating, speed skating, snowboarding, and skiing.

6. A new event at the 2002 Olympics was skeleton, a kind of bobsledding.

7. In 2002, Germany received the largest number of medals.

PRACTICE 2

Find the nouns in the following sentences. Underline the thirteen count nouns. Circle the nine noncount nouns. (*For help, see page 2 of the Handbook.*)

EXAMPLE

I bought a <u>chicken</u> and some (milk) at the <u>supermarket</u>.

1. All plants and animals require oxygen for life.

2. Many people believe that love is blind.

3. If homework is too difficult, students may become discouraged.

Copyright © 2003 by Pearson Education, Inc.

I

4. Paul went shopping and bought two new shirts, a hat, and some paint.

5. These suitcases are too small. We need to buy new luggage.

6. Sherry loves music. She learned a new song yesterday.

7. The roses in the garden need water twice a week.

8. A poodle is a dog with short, curly hair.

Copyright © 2003 by Pearson Education, Inc.

Find and underline fifty-nine pronouns in the following sentences. (*For help, see pages 3–4 of the Handbook.*)

EXAMPLE

<u>These</u> pants are too large for <u>me</u>.

1. **A:** Could you pick up my gray suit from the dry cleaner today? I need to wear it tomorrow.

   B: I'm really sorry, but this is a busy day for me. I'm afraid you'll have to pick it up yourself.

   A: That's impossible. I'm going to be in meetings from 8:00 a.m. until 6:00 p.m.

   B: Can you wear your dark blue suit instead of the gray one?

   A: Which dark blue suit?

   B: You know, the one that you got for your brother's wedding.

   A: Oh, *that* suit. I forgot all about it. It's kind of formal, don't you think?

   B: Maybe a little. But it looks wonderful on you.

2. People say that dogs and cats are natural enemies, but my dog, Ralph, and my cat, Rex, are very good friends. I got them two years ago from a friend who had to move to a different city. At first they were shy with me, but after a few days (and a few meals!), we all started to feel comfortable together.

   Ralph and Rex are both entertaining and interesting to watch. For example, they love to lick one another, and it's quite funny to watch them taking a "bath" this way. My pets also seem to enjoy looking at themselves in the mirror. I wonder: Do they recognize themselves, or do they think they're seeing a different cat and dog? Another one of their favorite activities is looking out

Copyright © 2003 by Pearson Education, Inc.

the front window. They get very excited whenever anybody walks by, especially if it's another dog or cat.

I don't know if animals have feelings like people do, but if they do, then it's clear that Ralph and Rex love each other. To tell you the truth, they get along better than a lot of people I know!

Copyright © 2003 by Pearson Education, Inc.

Find and underline all the verbs in the following sentences. Mark the main verbs *MV* and the helping verbs *HV*. Look for verbs in contractions, and mark the verb part of the contraction. There are twenty-nine main verbs and fourteen helping verbs. (*For help, see pages 4–7 of the Handbook.*)

EXAMPLE

<pre>
       MV   MV HV HV   MV
Today isn't a good day for a picnic. I think it's going to rain.
</pre>

1. **A:** You seem quiet this morning.

   B: Yeah, well, I'm worried about my mother.

   A: What happened to her?

   B: She broke her leg, and she's having a hard time getting around. I want to help her, but she says she's fine and she doesn't want any help.

   A: She sounds like a very independent person.

   B: Yes, she is. But ever since my father died, I know she's been pretty lonely.

2. **A:** Do you like sports?

   B: It depends. I like playing a few sports, and I like watching others.

   A: What do you like to play?

   B: Mainly volleyball and soccer. Oh, and swimming. I love to swim.

   A: Me too! In fact, I was planning to go to the pool tonight. Do you want to come too?

   B: What time are you planning to go? I have to finish a report for my literature class before I can do anything else.

   A: I was thinking about 8:00 p.m.

   B: Can you make it a little later, like 9:00?

   A: Sure. I'll come by at 9:00, and we'll walk over to the gym together.

Copyright © 2003 by Pearson Education, Inc.

Find and underline the adjectives (including nouns and pronouns used as adjectives) in the following sentences and draw an arrow to the word each one modifies. There are twenty-six adjectives. (*For help, see page 8 of the Handbook.*)

EXAMPLE

I live in a <u>small</u> <u>white</u> house with <u>large</u> windows and a <u>red</u> roof.

1. I work as a professional writer. I like to get up very early in the morning and write while the world is quiet and my mind is clear.

2. However, by 10:00 a.m., I'm usually ready for a break. Several times a week, I pack a newspaper, a small notebook, and some pencils, and I walk over to Josie's, a coffee shop near my home.

3. Going to Josie's is always a pleasant experience. During the ten-minute walk, I get a chance to breathe fresh air, say hello to my friendly neighbors, and enjoy the colorful gardens along the way.

4. As I approach Josie's, the heavenly smell of roasted coffee and cinnamon reaches my nose even before I open the door.

5. Josie's is furnished with tables and chairs for people who want to work while they drink. There are also soft, comfortable sofas where you can read and relax.

6. Spending time at Josie's helps me in my work. While I'm there, I can see interesting or unusual people, and I often overhear fascinating conversations.

Copyright © 2003 by Pearson Education, Inc.

Find and underline all the articles in the following sentences. There are seventeen indefinite articles and six definite articles. (*For help, see page 9 of the Handbook.*)

EXAMPLE

<u>The</u> refrigerator contained <u>a</u> bottle of wine, some milk, <u>an</u> old, half-eaten tuna

sandwich, and <u>a</u> bunch of grapes.

1. If you are a citizen of the United States, you must have a valid passport to

   travel overseas.

2. You do not need a visa to travel to most European or Latin American countries.

3. On the other hand, a visa is required for travel to many Asian countries, such

   as China, India, and Vietnam.

4. Most of the countries in the Middle East also require a visa.

5. To get a visa, it is necessary to fill out an application, submit a photo, and pay

   a fee.

6. A few countries will require you to have an AIDS test before you are allowed

   to enter the country.

7. If you travel overseas, it is a good idea to have medical insurance that will

   cover emergency medical needs.

8. The U.S. State Department has a list of English-speaking doctors in almost

   every country.

9. If you want to drive overseas, you might need to have an international driving

   permit. To get a permit, you must first have a valid U.S. driver's license.

10. U.S. citizens do not need to obtain an international driving permit to drive in

    Canada.

Copyright © 2003 by Pearson Education, Inc.

Find and underline twenty-one adverbs in the following sentences. Draw an arrow to the word each adverb modifies. (*For help, see pages 9–10 of the Handbook.*)

EXAMPLE

My English teacher <u>always</u> speaks <u>too</u> <u>fast</u>.

1. This morning I woke up very early because I had to take my best friend to the airport.

2. Please put the table here and the lamp over there.

3. I'm very sorry, but I have forgotten your name again.

4. Mr. Gregory almost always eats chicken for dinner.

5. He speaks English perfectly, Spanish fairly well, and Portuguese badly.

6. Some people were talking loudly in the hall, so I couldn't hear the lecture clearly.

7. The police officer cautiously approached the suspicious object near the park bench.

8. A large group of people stood outside, waiting patiently for the post office doors to open at 8:00 a.m.

9. It is important to change your pet bird's water daily.

10. I've been feeling very tired lately. I really need a vacation.

Copyright © 2003 by Pearson Education, Inc.

Find and underline thirty-six prepositions in the following sentences. (*For help, see pages 11–12 of the Handbook.*)

EXAMPLE

<u>For</u> my sister's birthday, I took her <u>to</u> lunch <u>at</u> the most expensive restaurant <u>in</u> town.

1. Linda Nelson and her husband, Martin, both work at home part of the time.

2. They used to share an office inside their house. However, this led to many arguments because of their different personalities and work styles.

3. Linda is a tidy and organized person. Her files are always in order, her books are lined up in neat rows, and there are never papers on the floor. When she finishes working, she always puts everything away. There is nothing on her desk except for a lamp, a box of pencils, and a tray for her unanswered mail.

4. Martin, unlike Linda, is messy and disorganized. In his work area, there are papers on chairs, books under the table, and notes taped to the walls. His computer screen is covered with fingerprints, and there is dust on all the furniture.

5. When Martin and Linda shared an office in the house, they were frequently angry with each other. Each of them wanted the other person to change, yet neither of them was capable of doing so. Clearly, sharing an office was not good for their marriage.

6. Fortunately, they were able to come up with a solution to the problem.

7. They went to the bank and took out a loan of $20,000.

8. With this money, they built an office for Martin above their garage.

9. Now Linda does not have to deal with his messiness, and Martin does not have to deal with her criticism.

Copyright © 2003 by Pearson Education, Inc.

Find and underline twenty-one conjunctions in the following sentences. (*For help, see pages 12–15 of the Handbook.*)

EXAMPLE

<u>Although</u> I live in a large city, I meet friends <u>wherever</u> I go.

1. Calcium (Ca) is the mineral in the human body that makes up our bones and keeps them strong.

2. It is essential not only for children but also for adults.

3. Our bodies store calcium in our bones and teeth, and we can protect this stored calcium by eating foods containing calcium.

4. Unless we eat enough calcium, however, the body automatically takes the calcium it needs from our bones.

5. Over the years, if we use up more calcium than we take in, our bones will become soft and break easily. Then we may get a disease called osteoporosis.

6. Adults aged 19 to 50 need about 1,000 mg per day of calcium, whereas children aged 1 to 18 need from 500 to 1,300 mg.

7. Which foods should we eat so that we can get all the calcium we need?

8. The best source of calcium is milk, but many people dislike the taste of milk.

9. Besides, milk is both high in calories and hard for many people to digest.

10. Consequently, some people prefer to get their calcium from other dairy sources, such as yogurt and cheese.

11. People who cannot eat dairy products at all can get the calcium they need from vegetables such as broccoli and kale. Salmon and tofu are also extremely high in calcium.

Copyright © 2003 by Pearson Education, Inc.

3b Dependent clauses

Underline seventeen dependent clauses in the following conversation. One sentence has no dependent clause. (*For help, see pages 19–21 of the Handbook.*)

EXAMPLE

It's easier to understand a country's culture <u>when you know its history</u>.

1. **SHARON:** Jack's twenty-first birthday is on Saturday, and we're planning a surprise party for that night. Let's decide how we are going to divide up the work.

2. **MAX:** What are the things that need to be done?

3. **SHARON:** Well, we need to clean the apartment, send out invitations, buy food, and get the drinks. Oh, and we need to find someone who will bring Jack to the party.

4. **MARTA:** I can do that. I'm taking Jack to a movie that afternoon, and afterwards we're going to have dinner. While we're eating, the guests can come over and help to set everything up. After Jack and I finish eating, I'll say that I need to stop by your apartment because I left my guitar there. And as soon as we arrive, everybody will shout, "Surprise!"

5. **SHARON:** That's a great plan. OK, now let's decide what we're going to eat and drink. Of course we need a cake.

6. **MAX:** I'll get that if you tell me where to buy it.

7. **SHARON:** Do you know where the Cake Factory is? It's the bakery where Sofie's mother works. But go early in the morning so that you can find a parking place.

Copyright © 2003 by Pearson Education, Inc.

8. MAX: OK, no problem. What about drinks?

9. SHARON: I'll ask Sofie to bring juice and soft drinks. If people want beer or wine, they can bring their own.

10. MAX: I suggest that we also have snacks like chips and nuts and maybe some fruit.

11. SHARON: When I call the guests, I'll ask each of them to bring something.

Copyright © 2003 by Pearson Education, Inc.

Underline the complete subject and write *SS* above the simple subject of each sentence. In some sentences, the subject has two parts. (*For help, see pages 22–23 of the Handbook.*)

EXAMPLE

         SS

The Mediterranean monk seal is one of the

most endangered animals on earth.

1. At one time, thousands of these animals could be found on beaches and in

   caves all around the Mediterranean Sea.

2. Now only an estimated 300 to 500 of them remain.

3. The remaining seals live in two main colonies, one in the eastern

   Mediterranean and the other in the western coast of Africa.

4. In the past, hunting for the seals' skins was the main reason for the decline of

   the seal population.

5. More recently, the greatest threats have been destruction of the animals by

   fishermen and disturbance of the seals' last remaining habitats (caves with

   underwater entrances) by swimmers and scuba divers.

6. A variety of national laws and species-protection programs have been created

   to protect the Mediterranean monk seal.

7. Protected areas have been established by Greece, Madeira, and Mauritania.

8. Because the seals are both rare and very shy, the number of people who have

   ever seen one of these beautiful creatures is extremely small.

9. If nations do not take care to preserve the Mediterranean monk seal, a unique

   natural treasure will be lost forever.

Copyright © 2003 by Pearson Education, Inc.

PART 2 Clear Sentences

6a Making compound sentences

Combine each pair of sentences with the connector that best fits the meaning. Be sure to use correct punctuation. (*For help, see pages 33–36 of the Handbook.*)

EXAMPLE

Janet is quite health-conscious. She rarely eats sweets. (*for/however/so*)

Janet is quite health-conscious, so she rarely eats sweets.

_____

1. Many people believe the myth that bats suck people's blood. They are terrified of bats. (*but/as a result/in fact*)

_____

_____

2. In fact, most species of bats do not eat blood. They do not carry the disease rabies, another common myth. (*nor/furthermore/for example*)

_____

_____

3. Seventy percent of the world's bat species eat only insects. They are extremely helpful animals. (*similarly/so/yet*)

_____

_____

4. In the winter, bats in cold climates migrate to warmer places. They hibernate in caves. (*in contrast/or/meanwhile*)

_____

_____

  Copyright © 2003 by Pearson Education, Inc.

5. A small percentage of bats feed on the blood of warm-blooded animals such as birds, horses, and cattle. They are called "vampire" bats. (*still/but/; *)

_____

_____

6. Vampire bats are extremely rare. They are the most famous type of bat. (*yet/in addition/for instance*)

_____

_____

7. Another myth about bats is that they sometimes fly into people's hair. This is also completely untrue. (*however/subsequently/so*)

_____

_____

8. Bats, like humans, are warm-blooded mammals. They have hair and give birth to living young. (*but/so/moreover*)

_____

_____

9. Most bats are very small, weighing less than 100 grams. They can live as long as thirty years. (*for example/nor/nevertheless*)

_____

_____

10. Bats, which are fascinating animals, are not dangerous. They are not aggressive. (*and/nor/on the other hand*)

_____

_____

Copyright © 2003 by Pearson Education, Inc.

Fill in each blank with a coordinating conjunction that fits the context. Use *and, or, but,* or *yet.* There is more than one possible answer for items 1 and 9. (*For help, see pages 37–38 of the Handbook.*)

EXAMPLE

The foolish boys didn't take a map, a flashlight, _____*or*_____ a cell phone on their hike.

My ten-year-old daughter, Gayle, has unusual eating habits. First, she is very selective about the foods she eats. For example, she likes yogurt (1) _____ not milk (2) _____ cheese. She hates fish (3) _____ most kinds of meat. She also dislikes cooked vegetables—except for broccoli! Fortunately, she loves salad, carrots, (4) _____ every kind of fruit. She also likes rice, pasta, (5) _____ tofu. Unlike most children her age, she dislikes candy (6) _____ chocolate.

Gayle's food preferences are not only strange but also unpredictable. Sometimes she eats chicken for breakfast (7) _____ cereal for dinner. For a snack after school she might ask for popcorn, a whole tomato, (8) _____ a slice of pizza. I never know what to expect.

Gayle has strange eating habits, (9) _____ she is not fat (10) _____ sick. In fact, she is very healthy because she seldom eats sweets (11) _____ "junk" food.

Copyright © 2003 by Pearson Education, Inc.

6c Connecting words with correlative conjunctions

Fill in each blank with a paired conjunction that fits the context. Use *both . . . and, not only . . . but also, either . . . or, neither . . . nor, whether . . . or.* Some items have more than one possible answer. (*For help, see pages 38–39 of the Handbook.*)

EXAMPLE

To get to the city center from here, you can _____*either*_____ catch a streetcar

at the corner _____*or*_____ walk two blocks to the subway station.

I grew up in a large, noisy, happy family. I had one older sister and two older

brothers, so I was the "baby." My mother and my father worked full time, so

all of us were expected (**1**) _____ to take care of ourselves

(**2**) _____ to help around the house. We learned to be independent

at a very young age.

Weekdays were very busy in our house. Everybody had to get up, get dressed,

eat breakfast, and leave the house by 7:30 a.m. To get to school, we kids

could (**3**) _____ walk (**4**) _____ ride our bicycles.

(**5**) _____ my sister (**6**) _____ my brothers played sports

after school. They used to come home around 5:30 p.m. Then everybody helped

to cook dinner and clean up, and after dinner, we (**7**) _____ did our

homework, watched TV, (**8**) _____ spent time in our rooms.

Saturday was also a busy day for us. My parents expected us

(**9**) _____ to do our homework (**10**) _____ to clean our

rooms. After our work was done, we could decide (**11**) _____ to get

together with friends (**12**) _____ to spend time at home. Sunday was

Copyright © 2003 by Pearson Education, Inc.

my family's day of rest. We always went to church in the morning. After that, we were free for the rest of the day.

My parents worked hard and sacrificed a lot for us kids. They rarely went out to a movie or took a vacation alone. Yet as far as I can remember, (13) _____ my mother (14) _____ my father ever complained. They sacrificed willingly because they loved us so much.

Copyright © 2003 by Pearson Education, Inc.

Edit the sentences in this letter for eight mistakes in parallel form. Some sentences have no errors. (*For help, see pages 40–41 of the Handbook.*)

EXAMPLE

its eventual space needs.

When choosing a pet, consider the pet's growth and ~~how much space it will~~

~~eventually need~~.

To Whom It May Concern:

It is my pleasure to write this letter of recommendation for Ms. Maria Castro, who was a student in my American Short Stories for International Students course during the spring semester of 2003. The course required students to read famous American short stories and interacting with the texts. In all areas—reading, speaking, and write—Maria was one of the best students I have ever had. Her comments, not only in speaking but also written, were original, intelligent, and they were often funny. Whenever I asked a question in class, Maria usually had an answer, yet listened carefully to other students' ideas too. Therefore, Maria was well-liked and she was admired by her classmates. Because of her intelligence, her strong motivation to learn, and she has excellent language skills, I am confident Maria can succeed as a full-time student at your university.

If you have additional questions about this student, I would be happy to answer them. Please feel free to contact me either by phone or you can send me an e-mail.

Sincerely yours,

Rosemary Becker, English Instructor

Copyright © 2003 by Pearson Education, Inc.

PRACTICE I

A. Insert the adverbs from the box in the appropriate places in the following paragraph. (*For help, see pages 42–45 of the Handbook.*)

EXAMPLE

The bus left _____*as soon as*_____ I got on.

as soon as	although	when	so that	if	after

John and his best friend, Thomas, will both graduate from high school next

spring. **(1)** _____ both of them are excellent students, they plan

to do different things **(2)** _____ they graduate. John, who wants

to be an engineer, plans to start college **(3)** _____ he graduates.

He wants to finish college as quickly as possible **(4)** _____ he can

start working at his father's engineering firm. Thomas, on the other hand, wants

to join the army **(5)** _____ he graduates. He thinks that

(6) _____ he serves in the army first, he can learn useful skills

and figure out what he wants to study in college.

B. Edit the following sentences for adverb clause errors. Every sentence has an error. (*For help, see pages 42–45 of the Handbook.*)

EXAMPLE

Jorge didn't pass the exam~~X~~ ᵇBecause he forgot to study.

1. Don't leave the door open. If the air conditioner is turned on.

2. Because I misplaced my car keys, so I wasn't able to go out today.

3. Please wash the dishes after you put them away in the cupboard.

4. While the professor spoke, then the students took notes.

Copyright © 2003 by Pearson Education, Inc.

5. My mother said, "Until you finish your homework, you can watch half an hour

of television."

6. We don't need to go to school today, because it's Saturday.

PRACTICE 2

Underline the adjective clauses in the following paragraphs, and draw an arrow
to the antecedent of each. Circle the relative pronoun or adverb. There are ten
adjective clauses in the four paragraphs. (*For help, see page 46 of the Handbook.*)

EXAMPLE

The Hawaiian Islands, which comprise 8 major and 124 minor islands, became

the fiftieth state of the United States in 1959.

Vatican City, which has an area of only 0.2 square mile, is generally considered

to be the world's smallest country. Yet some people say there is a country that is

even smaller than the Vatican. You have probably never heard of it. It is called

the Sovereign Military Order of Malta (SMOM). Although it was once an

independent country, today it is principally a religious organization that provides

humanitarian and medical assistance all over the world.

The Order of Malta was founded in 1099, when it established a hospital in

Jerusalem to care for sick travelers during the First Crusade. The organization

later expanded and built additional hospitals along the route from Europe to the

Holy Land. In 1530 it was given the island of Malta, from which it got its name. In

1834 the organization moved to Rome, where it still has its headquarters today.

The Order of Malta currently has about 5,000 members. It is governed by a

"Grand Master" and a "Sovereign Council," which has both permanent and elected

members who accept the authority of the Pope and the Roman Catholic Church.

Copyright © 2003 by Pearson Education, Inc.

Although the order has no territory other than its headquarters in Rome and a fortress in Malta, it is officially recognized by 67 countries. It makes coins, which do not circulate, and it prints stamps that are accepted by 45 national post offices. It has been a permanent observer at the United Nations since 1994. Thus, it is unclear whether the Order of Malta can be called the world's smallest nation or not.

PRACTICE 3

A. Find and underline seven noun clauses in the following paragraph. (*For help, see pages 47–48 of the Handbook.*)

EXAMPLE

Our English teacher announced <u>that we would have a vocabulary test on Friday</u>.

Ms. Angela White is one of the most respected teachers in our school for several reasons. First, she takes the time to find out who her students are and what they are interested in, and she tries to connect her lessons to her students' lives and interests. Second, her students say that she is very fair. She makes sure that every person in her class gets an equal chance to participate, and she never plays favorites. Next, Ms. White always gives clear instructions so that students understand exactly what they are supposed to do. In addition, she is sensitive to her students' feelings. If they make mistakes, she knows how to correct them so that students do not feel ashamed. One last thing that makes Ms. White such a good teacher is her nice voice. Her students always mention how much they enjoy listening to her.

Copyright © 2003 by Pearson Education, Inc.

B. Edit the noun clauses in the following sentences for mistakes. There are seven errors. (*For help, see pages 47–48 of the Handbook.*)

EXAMPLE

My parents decided that I should become a businessman without asking me
ed
what d̶i̶d̶ I want˄to do with my life.

1. Do you know what is the homework for Monday?

2. **A:** Excuse me, I'm trying to find the post office. Can you tell me, how to get

 there?

 B: Sure. It's at the corner of Olympic Boulevard and First Street. Do you

 know where is that?

 A: Yes, I do. Thanks for your help.

3. I don't know who directed the movie *Titanic?*

4. If we want to get good seats for the concert, it's essential that we are at the

 auditorium no later than 7:00 p.m.

5. Excuse me, can you tell me what time is it?

Copyright © 2003 by Pearson Education, Inc.

A. Circle the appositives and appositive phrases in the following paragraphs, and draw an arrow to the nouns or noun phrases they rename. (*For help, see page 49 of the Handbook.*)

EXAMPLE

The cellist (Pablo Casals) died in 1973 at the age of 97.

The composer Wolfgang Amadeus Mozart is regarded as one of the greatest musical geniuses who ever lived. He was born in 1756 in the Austrian town of Salzburg, a stunningly beautiful city with a long musical history. Mozart's musical gifts became obvious almost immediately. By the age of four, he could already play the piano. He published his first compositions, four pieces for violin and harpsichord, before his eighth birthday.

Mozart's father, Leopold, had been a music teacher. However, he quit teaching to manage young Wolfgang's career. When Mozart was six, he began playing concerts with his sister, Nanerl, who was also a gifted musician. At the age of seven, Mozart was invited to Vienna, the capital of Austria, to play for the royal family. From there, his reputation as a genius spread all over Europe.

B. Combine each pair of sentences on page 24 into one sentence. Make the second sentence an appositive or appositive phrase, and insert it into the first sentence. Add commas if the appositive is extra information. One item has no appositive, and one item has two. (*For help, see page 49 of the Handbook.*)

EXAMPLE

Mozart's first public performance took place in Munich. Munich is a city in southern Germany.

Mozart's first public performance took place in Munich, a city in southern

Germany.

Copyright © 2003 by Pearson Education, Inc.

1. In 1984, a mostly fictional account of Mozart's life was told in a film. The film was *Amadeus*.

   _____

   _____

2. Much of the film focused on Mozart's rivalry with another composer. The composer was Salieri.

   _____

   _____

3. At the end of the movie, Salieri poisons Mozart. Salieri was jealous of Mozart's genius.

   _____

   _____

4. In fact, the cause of Mozart's death at age 35 is not certain. It may have been a fever or a medical condition. The condition is uremia. Uremia is a result of advanced kidney disease.

   _____

   _____

5. Mozart died before completing his last masterpiece. The piece was his unforgettable *Requiem*.

   _____

   _____

Copyright © 2003 by Pearson Education, Inc.

Shorten adjective and adverb clauses whenever possible in the following sentences. Some sentences have more than one clause that can be reduced. There are thirteen clauses that can be shortened. (*For help, see pages 51–52 of the Handbook.*)

EXAMPLE

Having a bad cold
~~Because I had a bad cold~~, I could not smell the meat ~~that was~~ burning in

the oven.

1. I had never experienced an earthquake before I visited California.

2. Because she was frightened of water, Mrs. Alvarez never went swimming with

   her children.

3. While I was working at home one day, I received a phone call from a man

   who told me I had won $10,000 in a contest.

4. Towns that are located near rivers must be prepared for floods in the

   springtime.

5. When you are eating fish, you should be careful not to swallow any small bones.

6. A person who wishes to practice law in the United States must first pass a

   difficult examination that is known as the bar exam.

7. The blond woman, who didn't realize someone else was in the room, picked

   up a silver letter opener and put it in her purse.

8. I enjoyed watching the children who were playing baseball in the park.

9. Even after he had lived in the United States for 25 years, my father still had a

   heavy accent when he spoke English.

10. The man who was arrested by the police was wanted for robbing banks in

    three cities.

  Copyright © 2003 by Pearson Education, Inc.

A. There are five fragments in the following paragraph. Find and correct them. There is more than one way to make the corrections. The first fragment has been corrected as an example. (*For help, see pages 54–56 of the Handbook.*)

Los Angeles is a multinational city with immigrants from all over the world.

Many of these immigrants live in "ethnic" neighborhoods. For example,

                    i
Chinatown/~~I~~s a unique community of approximately 14,000 people. Chinese

culture dominates the area. Have Chinese restaurants, clothing stores, bakeries,

banks, bookstores, gift shops, jewelers, markets, beauty salons, and more. Some of

Chinatown's residents have lived there for forty or fifty years, and they have never

learned much English. Because they haven't needed it. Is possible to get almost any

Chinese product or service in Chinatown. Without traveling to China.

B. Find and correct five fragments in the following paragraph. (*For help, see pages 54–56 of the Handbook.*)

Los Angeles is an enjoyable city to visit. If you have a car. If not, you will need

to depend on public transportation. Which is neither fast nor convenient.

Los Angeles has a new subway, but it does not travel to most of the popular

tourist attractions. There is no system of elevated trains or streetcars. Only buses,

and they can take a long time to go anywhere. Because traffic is very heavy.

Especially in the early morning and late afternoon, when people are traveling

to and from work.

Copyright © 2003 by Pearson Education, Inc.

Some of the following items contain run-together sentences. Find the errors and correct them, using any appropriate technique. There is more than one way to make corrections. (*For help, see pages 57–58 of the Handbook.*)

EXAMPLE

On Sunday we worked in the garden⊙ᴸ later we went to a baseball game.

1. Broccoli is an ancient vegetable, it has been around for more than 2,000 years.

2. The word *broccoli* comes from the Italian word *brocco*, it means an arm or a branch.

3. It is one of the healthiest vegetables it is rich in vitamins and low in calories.

4. Surprisingly, it has as much calcium as an equal amount of milk.

5. Broccoli contains a special chemical substance called sulforaphane, it helps reduce the risk of cancer.

6. Broccoli normally grows best in cool climates recently new varieties that grow well in mild and subtropical climates have been developed in Taiwan.

7. Most broccoli varieties are green, however, there are a few that are purple in color.

8. Broccoli is one of the most popular vegetables in the United States, not everyone likes it, however.

9. One famous broccoli hater is George Bush, he was president of the United States from 1989 to 1993.

10. President Bush angered American broccoli growers when he said, "I do not like broccoli. . . . Now I'm President of the United States, and I'm not going to eat any more broccoli."

Copyright © 2003 by Pearson Education, Inc.

The following letter contains choppy writing. Improve it by combining sentences using coordination and subordination. One revision has been made as an example. (*For help, see page 59 of the Handbook.*)

Mrs. Charlene Goren

Director, English Language Institute

5893 Key Ave.

Any City, USA   November 13, 200_

Dear Mrs. Goren:

I am a student here at the English Language Institute. I would like to make some

        that

suggestions,/~~They~~ will make this school more pleasant and convenient for all the

students.

My first suggestion is that you should build a dormitory next to the school

building. We are overseas students. We live far from the school. Most of us do not

have cars. It would be better for us to have rooms close to the school. That would

reduce the problems of absence and tardiness.

In addition, you should open a cafeteria in the building. It should have a variety of

food and music. It would be convenient. It would be relaxing. Students and

teachers could eat together. They could get to know one another better.

You should also add a library. It will help us in our studies.

Fourth, it would be very nice if the building had new paint. It would make the

building more attractive. It would give new students a more positive first

impression of the school. It would reflect the excellent education that students

can get here.

Copyright © 2003 by Pearson Education, Inc.   **29**

I hope that these suggestions will receive your approval. They will improve student life at the English Language Institute. They will help to attract new students.

Thank you for your attention.

Sincerely,

Kofi Attitso (from Ghana)

Copyright © 2003 by Pearson Education, Inc.

The following student essay is an example of the overuse of *and, but,* and *so.* Improve the essay using any appropriate technique. The first revision has been made as an example. (*For help, see pages 60–61 of the Handbook.*)

⊙ *Although*
My wife and I were married at the age of 21/~~and~~ we have always loved each

other, ~~but~~ I think it was a mistake to get married at such a young age. At the time

of our marriage, we were still university students, and our parents advised us to

wait until graduation to get married, but we did not want to wait, so we ignored

our parents' advice, and in the early years of our marriage, we had many

problems.

Both of us had lived at home until our marriage, so we did not have any

experience living independently, and we did not know how to shop or cook or clean

or make decisions for ourselves. Our parents agreed to continue paying for our

education, but we had to pay for our apartment and food, so both of us had to get

part-time jobs, and we were exhausted all the time, and we had many arguments.

Many couples in our situation would have gotten divorced, but we were lucky

and we stayed together in spite of our problems. Both of us graduated from the

university and got good jobs. Then we had more time and more money, so we

didn't argue so much and we really began to enjoy our lives together. Now we are

expecting our first baby, and we feel very happy and grateful for our good fortune.

Copyright © 2003 by Pearson Education, Inc.

A. Edit the following sentences for errors in word order. (*For help, see pages 62–64 of the Handbook.*)

EXAMPLE

We watched a video last night at home.

1. The little girl opened quickly her birthday presents.

2. I had studied harder in high school, I might have been accepted at a better university.

3. After graduating from college, my best friend and I traveled for three months in Europe and North Africa.

4. Rarely Blanca does drink more than one cup of coffee per day.

5. How long you have lived in Canada?

6. While working in the back of the house, I heard my doorbell ring. I went to open the door. Stood on the front porch a delivery man holding an enormous box. "You are Rosemary Baxter?" asked he. "No," I replied. "Next door she lives."

B. In the following items, use all the elements to compose sentences with correct word order. (*For help, see pages 62–64 of the Handbook.*)

EXAMPLE

at 12 o'clock / everyone / goes / to lunch / in my office
Everyone in my office goes to lunch at 12 o'clock.

1. every week / there / new students / are / in my class / nearly

_____

2. tourists / visit / seldom / our small town / do / in the winter

_____

Copyright © 2003 by Pearson Education, Inc.

3. you / please / need / do / should / any help / not / to ask / hesitate

_____

4. has / India / how long / been / an independent country?

_____

5. difficult / for me / it / early / is / to get up / in the morning

_____

6. often / we / breakfast / on weekends / in bed / eat

_____

Copyright © 2003 by Pearson Education, Inc.

A. Rewrite the following sentences so that they include the prepositions *for* or *to*. (*For help, see pages 65–66 of the Handbook.*)

EXAMPLE

When my roommate graduated, she sold me her car.

When my roommate graduated, she sold her car to me.

1. Could you please make me a cup of tea?

   _____

2. As soon as I walked into the house, my husband handed me an important-looking letter.

   _____

3. Every year on my birthday, my mother cooks me all my favorite dishes.

   _____

4. Could you do me a big favor? Would you mind lending me your car?

   _____

5. While I was away at college, my boyfriend sent me an e-mail message every day.

   _____

6. If you're going to the supermarket, could you please get me some milk?

   _____

7. George, who is an excellent carpenter, built his daughter a treehouse in the backyard.

   _____

8. Mr. Chin got himself a new suit when he was in London.

   _____

Copyright © 2003 by Pearson Education, Inc.

9. My boss asked me to show her the report before I mailed it to the customer.

_____

10. If the product you buy is defective, most stores will refund you your money.

_____

B. Find and correct six errors in the following paragraph. (*For help, see pages 65–66 of the Handbook.*)

EXAMPLE

My teacher recommended to me a good book

Last night my roommate introduced me one of her classmates. She said me his name, but I couldn't hear it. "What?" I asked. Then my roommate pronounced me his name, but I still couldn't get it.

"Could you repeat me it again?" I asked him.

"Sure. It's Jedidiah. But you can just call me Jed, OK?"

"OK," I replied. "What does your name mean? Can you translate me it?"

"It means 'Friend of God' in the Hebrew language."

"That's beautiful," I replied. "Thank you for explaining me your name."

Copyright © 2003 by Pearson Education, Inc.

Improve this story by beginning at least ten sentences with an element other than the subject. Write your edited story on a separate sheet of paper. (*For help, see pages 66–68 of the Handbook.*)

EXAMPLE

We spend a month at the beach every summer.

Every summer we spend a month at the beach.

I want to tell you the remarkable story of how I met my best friend, Max.

My family lives in New York City, and we own a beach house on Long Island. We spend a month there every summer, swimming, fishing, and just hanging out on the beach. My cousins were visiting seven years ago, and one day we decided to try something we had seen in a movie. We found an empty wine bottle first. We took a piece of paper after that, and we wrote down our names, addresses, and ages. I wrote an additional message since I was the oldest, asking the person who found the bottle to please call me either on Long Island or in New York.

Then my cousins and I sailed out into the Atlantic Ocean and dropped the bottle in the water about two miles from the shore. We watched it drift away slowly, wondering when and by whom it would be found.

We searched the beach every morning from then until the end of our vacation to see if the bottle had miraculously returned during the night. Of course it did not. Summer ended, we returned to the city, school began, and eventually we forgot all about the bottle.

I was doing my homework one evening about two years later when the telephone rang. I picked it up absentmindedly and said, "Hello?" A woman's voice replied "'Allo? You are Max Waller?" She had a clear French accent. I told her excitedly that yes, I was Max Waller. She said she had found a bottle on the beach containing my name and address and a request to call. She then said the most astonishing thing of all: She had a son whose name was also Max who was just about my age, and he was learning English in school.

I had just started taking French in school, amazingly. The other Max and I spoke a few words on the phone and exchanged e-mail addresses. We became penpals in this way. We wrote to each other regularly for the next five years. We also spoke on the phone from time to time.

Max and I are finally going to meet now, five years later. Both of us are going to graduate from high school this June, and our parents are going to give us the same gift: the opportunity to visit each other in our home countries. Max will come here from France on June 20 and stay with my family at the beach for one month. I will return to France with him for a month after that.

In the fall both of us are going to start our university studies. Can you guess what each of us plans to study? I, predictably, am going to major in French. And Max is going to major in . . . economics!

36

Copyright © 2003 by Pearson Education, Inc.

Edit the following sentences for gender-sensitive language, informal language, and slang. (*For help, see pages 69–72 of the Handbook.*)

EXAMPLE

or her

Each student is responsible for cleaning up his own trash.   OR

All students are   *their*

~~Each student is~~ responsible for cleaning up ~~his~~ own trash.

1. Cindy, please put this letter outside in the mailbox so that the mailman can

   pick it up tomorrow.

2. (At an executive business meeting, the company president is speaking.) "Please

   chill out, you guys, because it's time for us to get this show on the road."

3. Peter's mommy is a dentist, and his daddy is a photographer.

4. I was very thirsty, so I asked the stewardess to bring me a glass of orange juice.

5. If a person wants to become a policeman, he must graduate from the police

   academy and spend two years under the direct supervision of an experienced

   cop.

6. STUDENT: Hey, man, can I make an appointment to talk to you after school?

   TEACHER: What do you want to talk about?

   STUDENT: Well, I really tanked on[1] the last math exam.

   TEACHER: I dig.[2] All right, why don't you come to my office at 3:15?

7. In the United States, a kindergarten teacher must have a college education. She

   is also required to do at least one year of supervised teaching before she can

   teach a class by herself.

---

[1]**tanked on** (slang): got a low score
[2]**I dig** (slang): I see or I understand

Copyright © 2003 by Pearson Education, Inc.

8. These days security at airports is very strict. Therefore, every airline passenger has to have his or her bags checked before he or she is allowed to enter the boarding area.

9. Most waitresses earn only about $5.00 an hour. They depend on tips from their customers to make a decent living.

Copyright © 2003 by Pearson Education, Inc.

11b Verb tenses

PRACTICE I

Complete each sentence with the correct form of the verbs in parentheses. Choose between the simple present and the present progressive. The subject is provided if necessary. (*For help, see pages 76–80 of the Handbook.*)

EXAMPLE

John _____*owns*_____ (*own*) a car, but these days he

_____*is riding*_____ (*ride*) his bicycle to work.

I (**1**) _____ (*sit*) at a corner table in a restaurant, and I

(**2**) _____ (*watch*) a middle-aged man and woman who

(**3**) _____ (*have*) lunch at the table next to me. The woman

(**4**) _____ (*have*) dyed blond hair and (**5**) _____

(*look*) about fifty. She (**6**) _____ (*drink*) coffee and

(**7**) _____ (*say*) something to the man, who

(**8**) _____ (*have*) gray hair and (**9**) _____ (*be*)

quite elegant looking. However, he (**10**) _____ (*not pay*)

attention to what she (**11**) _____ (*say*). Instead, he

(**12**) _____ (*watch closely*) the waitress, who

(**13**) _____ (*be*) busy serving other customers. Now the

man (**14**) _____ (*whisper*) something to the woman. She

(**15**) _____ (*appear*) displeased. Wait! What

(**16**) _____ (*they do*)? They (**17**) _____ (*get up*)

and (**18**) _____ (*walk*) toward the door! But the waitress, who

Copyright © 2003 by Pearson Education, Inc.

apparently (**19**) _____ (*have*) eyes in the back of her head,

(**20**) _____ (*run*) after them and (**21**) _____

(*call*), "Oh, sir, sir. Here is your check!"

PRACTICE 2

A. Complete the following paragraphs with either the present perfect or the present perfect progressive form of the verbs in parentheses. In some cases, both tenses are correct. (*For help, see pages 81–83 of the Handbook.*)

EXAMPLE

You ___*haven't called*___ (*not call*) me in over a week!

People around the world (**1**) _____ (*sight*) unidentified

flying objects (UFOs) for many years, but the number of sightings

(**2**) _____ (*increase*) in recent months. Government investigators

(**3**) _____ (*work*) overtime to check out all the reports,

which (**4**) _____ (*pour*) in from all parts of the globe.

People (**5**) _____ (*report*) not only sightings but also actual

physical contact with visitors from other planets. One man reported that he had

actually been taken aboard a UFO, examined, and then released. Although

government experts (**6**) _____ (*investigate*) the incident since it

happened, they (**7**) _____ (*not be able*) to either prove or

disprove it.

Government officials (**8**) _____ (*prepare*) a report on UFOs

for several months, but they (**9**) _____ (*not complete*) it yet

because they (**10**) _____ (*solve*) only two-thirds of the reported

Copyright © 2003 by Pearson Education, Inc.

sightings so far. As expected, all the sightings they (**11**) _____

(*investigate*) until now (**12**) _____ (*have*) perfectly logical

explanations.

B. Edit the following sentences for errors involving the present perfect or present perfect progressive. (*For help, see pages 81–83 of the Handbook.*)

EXAMPLE
has been
She ~~is~~ here since August 9.

1. Jack has always been loving music.

2. He has been taking piano lessons since four years.

3. This year he have gone to three classical performances.

4. He has also attending several rock and pop concerts.

5. He has never been going to a jazz concert, however.

PRACTICE 3

Complete each sentence with the correct form of the verb in parentheses. Other words are provided if necessary. There is more than one correct answer for some sentences. (*For help, see pages 84–86 of the Handbook.*)

A. In the following sentences, choose between the simple past and past progressive.

EXAMPLE

I _____*was talking*_____ (*talk*) on the phone when someone

_____*rang*_____ (*ring*) the doorbell.

1. John attends English classes every day from 9:00 a.m. to 12:00 p.m.

   Yesterday morning his mother _____ (*call*) him at

   11:30 a.m. Of course he _____ (*not answer*) the

Copyright © 2003 by Pearson Education, Inc.

phone because he _____ (*attend*) class at that

time, so she _____ (*leave*) a message.

2. **A:**   What _____ (*happen*) to Chris?

   B: While he _____ (*yawn*), a fly _____ (*fly*)

   into his mouth and he _____ (*swallow*) it!

3. Yesterday afternoon Jessica _____ (*lie*) on her bed and

_____ (*read*) a book. Suddenly she _____

(*hear*) a loud noise. She _____ (*get up*) and

_____ (*look*) out the window to see what it was.

Some workers _____ (*cut*) down a tree across the street.

B. In the following paragraph, choose among the simple past, present perfect, and present perfect progressive.

Julia is getting married in August. She (**1**) _____ (*plan*)

her wedding since she (**2**) _____ (*get*) engaged last

October, and her mother (**3**) _____ (*help*) her. They

(**4**) _____ (*not have*) any problems except that so far Julia

(**5**) _____ (*not find*) a wedding dress she likes. She and her

mother (**6**) _____ (*visit*) all the stores in town without success.

Julia (**7**) _____ (*tell*) her fiancé about her problem, and he

(**8**) _____ (*respond*), "Well, I (**9**) _____

(*never enjoy*) wearing a suit. Why don't we get married in blue jeans?"

Copyright © 2003 by Pearson Education, Inc.

PRACTICE 4

Complete each sentence with the correct form of the verbs in parentheses. Other words are provided if necessary. There is more than one correct answer for some sentences. (*For help, see pages 87–88 of the Handbook.*)

A. In the following sentences, choose between the simple past and past perfect.

EXAMPLE

She _____*ate*_____ (*eat*) a huge dinner because she

_____*had missed*_____ (*miss*) lunch.

1. I _____ (*just wash*) my car when it _____

(*begin*) to rain.

2. Heidi _____ (*be*) late to class this morning because she

_____ (*lose*) her watch and _____ (*not know*)

what time it was.

3. By the time Sonia _____ (*start*) college, she

_____ (*already have*) several part-time jobs. She

_____ (*work*) as a waitress, a store clerk, and a baby-sitter.

B. In the following sentences, choose among the simple past, past progressive, present perfect progressive, and past perfect progressive.

1. The students in Ms. Baker's English grammar class _____

(*wait*) for almost ten minutes when she finally _____ (*arrive*).

Ms. Baker _____ (*apologize*) and _____

(*explain*) that she _____ (*be*) in a car accident on the way

to work. She _____ (*wait*) at a red light when a car

Copyright © 2003 by Pearson Education, Inc.

_____ (*hit*) her from behind. Fortunately, she

_____ (*not be*) hurt.

2. It _____ (*snow*) since yesterday afternoon.

3. It _____ (*snow*) when I woke up this morning.

I _____ (*hear*) on the news that it _____

(*snow*) all night.

4. Jackie _____ (*live*) in the United States for almost six months

when her father _____ (*come*) for a visit. She

_____ (*not receive*) many letters from home, so she

_____ (*be*) eager to hear news about her family. Her father

_____ (*tell*) her that her mother _____ (*be*)

quite ill for several weeks during the summer, but she _____

(*recover*) completely by the time he _____ (*leave*) for the

United States.

PRACTICE 5

A. Complete each sentence with the correct form of the verbs in parentheses. Choose between the simple future, future perfect, and future (perfect) progressive. The first item is done as an example. (*For help, see pages 89–92 of the Handbook.*)

By the year 2020,

1. more nations _____*will be using*_____ (*use*) solar energy instead of oil.

2. doctors _____ (*be able*) to cure many diseases using

gene therapy.

3. tobacco _____ (*kill*) more people than any disease,

including HIV.

Copyright © 2003 by Pearson Education, Inc.

4. space shuttles _____ (*travel*) to and from earth for

almost forty years.

5. the world's population _____ (*grow*) to 7.5 billion.

B. Complete each sentence using either the future perfect or the future perfect progressive. The first item is done as an example. (*For help, see page 92 of the Handbook.*)

1. Ms. Tanaka began teaching English in 1995. By 2010, she

_____*will have been teaching*_____ for fifteen years.

2. James is on a diet. He has been losing about two pounds (one kilo) per week.

By the end of the month, he _____ about eight

pounds.

3. Judy and Joe were married in 1984. By 2009, they

_____ for twenty-five years.

4. Thomas started studying at 7:00 p.m. It is now 8:00 p.m. By 10:00 p.m., he

_____ for three hours.

C. Complete each sentence with any appropriate expression of future time. There is more than one correct answer for some sentences. (*For help, see pages 89–92 of the Handbook.*)

1. Hurry up! If we don't leave right now, we _____ (*be*) late!

2. Look at those clouds. It looks as if it _____ (*rain*) this

afternoon.

3. This class usually begins at 9:00 a.m., but tomorrow it _____

(*start*) at 10:00.

Copyright © 2003 by Pearson Education, Inc.

4. Next Friday night, we _____ (*go*) to a lecture about

Buddhism.

5. Where _____ (*you live*) at this time next year?

6. We have to be at the airport by noon because our flight _____

(*leave*) at 2:00.

PRACTICE 6

Edit the following paragraphs for incorrect verb tenses and unnecessary shifts
between present and past. There are nine mistakes. The first mistake has been
corrected for you as an example. (*For help, see page 93 of the Handbook.*)

A few days ago, while I was eating lunch in a small restaurant, I ~~overhear~~ an
overheard

interesting conversation. Two women, one of whom was pregnant, were sitting at a

table near me, and they are talking about baby names. The not-pregnant one asked if

the pregnant one and her husband have chosen names for the baby yet. The pregnant

one replied, "Well, if it's a boy, my husband wants to call him Robert Junior."

I didn't understand her answer. I learn in school that *junior* means "lower in

rank." I wonder why anyone would give this name to a baby. In my country,

China, we prefer names with a positive meaning.

I go home and look up *junior* in the dictionary. It explain that in the United

States, some families put the word *junior* after a boy's name if he has the same first

name as his father. This helped me to understand what the pregnant woman say.

Also, now I understood why two American presidents have the same name.

George Bush was the forty-first president of the United States, and George Bush

Junior, his son, was the forty-third.

Copyright © 2003 by Pearson Education, Inc.

PRACTICE I

Complete each sentence with the correct form of the verbs in parentheses. (*For help, see pages 94–95 of the Handbook.*)

EXAMPLE

I _____*need*_____ (*need*) to finish this report before I

_____*leave*_____ (*leave*) the office tonight.

1. I recently started my first job. Since I _____ (*start*) working,

   my life _____ (*change*) in a number of ways.

2. Before I _____ (*get*) my job, I always _____

   (*go*) to bed very late. Now I have to get up very early to catch the train to work.

3. Another thing that _____ (*change*) is my wardrobe.

   Before I _____ (*begin*) working, the only clothes I

   _____ (*own*) were casual pants, shirts, and sweaters.

4. I _____ (*become*) a much better dresser since I

   _____ (*join*) the workforce. I _____ (*spend*)

   hundreds of dollars buying new suits, shirts, and shoes that are suitable

   for the office. I even had to buy some ties!

5. Also, I used to go out with friends almost every night. Now, after I

   _____ (*finish*) working, I usually _____ (*go*)

   straight home. I don't have the time or the energy to stay out late.

6. Of course, weekends are different. For example, this Friday, as soon as the office

   _____ (*close*), I _____ (*meet*) my friends for

   dinner at our favorite restaurant.

Copyright © 2003 by Pearson Education, Inc.

7. After we _____ (*eat*), we _____ (*go*) dancing

at our favorite club.

8. I probably _____ (*not go*) home until the sun

_____ (*rise*). When I _____ (*get*) home,

I _____ (*eat*) some breakfast, and then I

_____ (*sleep*) until noon.

PRACTICE 2

A. Complete the conversation with the correct form of the verbs in parentheses. There is more than one correct answer for some of the items. (*For help, see pages 95–99 of the Handbook.*)

EXAMPLE

If I _____*had*_____ (*have*) a car, I ____*wouldn't need*____ (*not need*) to

take the bus to school.

MOTHER: Hurry up, Josh! It's 7:30! The bus is going to be here any second. If you

(**1**) _____ (*not hurry*), you (**2**) _____

(*miss*) the bus!

JOSH: I can't find my history book. Where did you put it?

MOTHER: Me? I never touched it! If you (**3**) _____ (*put*)

it in your backpack last night, you (**4**) _____

(*not need*) to be hunting for it now. I'm warning you: if you

(**5**) _____ (*miss*) the bus again, I

(**6**) _____ (*not drive*) you to school today. You

can walk!

Copyright © 2003 by Pearson Education, Inc.

JOSH: Walk? I **(7)** _____ (*be*) late for sure if I

(8) _____ (*have to walk*).

MOTHER: I'm sorry, Josh. I **(9)** _____ (*drive*) you if I

(10) _____ (*have*) time, but you know I have a job

and I can't be late to work. So please hurry up!

B. In the following sentences, find and correct six errors in the use of the conditional. One sentence has no errors. (*For help, see pages 95–99 of the Handbook.*)

EXAMPLE

I will cook dinner if you w~~ill~~ wash the dishes.

1. If I was a U.S. citizen, I would not need a visa to study at an American university.

2. Had I know it was going to rain, I would have taken an umbrella.

3. If Gina had gotten a higher score on the university entrance exam, she could have go to Harvard University.

4. If I have a better job, I could afford to buy a house instead of renting an apartment.

5. You must be talented and determined if you want to be a professional artist.

6. If you had to learn another language, which one will you choose?

7. I would have joined the swimming team if I had have more time.

Copyright © 2003 by Pearson Education, Inc.

PRACTICE 3

Complete the sentences with *unless, as long as, provided (that), in case,* or *in the event (that).* Use each expression at least once. You will need to use some expressions more than once. Some sentences have more than one correct answer. (*For help, see page 100 of the Handbook.*)

EXAMPLE

Be sure to take an umbrella _____*in case*_____ it rains tonight.

At City University there is not enough parking, and parking laws on campus are very strict.

1. You may not park on campus _____ you have a parking

   permit.

2. _____ you have a permit, you may park in any numbered

   parking lot.

3. The University Medical Center has its own parking lot. You may not park there

   _____ you are a patient, a visitor, or a hospital worker.

4. Sometimes all the parking spaces in a lot are taken. You should always arrive on

   campus early _____ you have to wait for a parking space.

5. _____ you have a permit, you will not get a parking ticket.

6. There are parking meters next to the bookstore. If you park there, you should

   always put extra money in the meter _____ you are delayed

   getting back to your car.

7. _____ you want to attend a concert or a lecture on campus

   but do not have a permit, you can buy a one-time parking pass for $5.00.

8. _____ you get a parking ticket, you will have thirty days to

   pay it.

Copyright © 2003 by Pearson Education, Inc.

PRACTICE 4

Change the dialogue into reported speech. Use each verb in the box at least once. (*For help, see pages 102–106 of the Handbook.*)

EXAMPLE

Ellen to Nancy: "I met a cool guy last night."

Ellen told Nancy that she had met a cool guy the night before.

inquire	add	explain	answer	say
ask		want to know	reply	conclude

1. Nancy: "Where did you meet him?"

   _____

2. Ellen: "I met him while I was standing in line at the supermarket last night."

   _____

3. Ellen: "He was nice looking and very charming."

   _____

4. Nancy: "Did you exchange phone numbers?"

   _____

5. Ellen: "He gave me his number and asked me to call him tomorrow."

   _____

6. Nancy: "Are you going to go out with him?"

   _____

7. Ellen: "I wish I could, but I can't."

   _____

Copyright © 2003 by Pearson Education, Inc.

8. Nancy: "Why?"

_____

9. Ellen: "He has a dog, and I'm allergic to dogs."

_____

10. Nancy: "In that case, maybe *I* should go out with him!"

_____

PRACTICE 5

A. Complete each sentence with the subjunctive form of the verbs in parentheses. Pay attention to the verbs and adjectives before the blanks. (*For help, see pages 106–107 of the Handbook.*)

EXAMPLE

If you have a question about your visa, I suggest that you

_____*make*_____ (*make*) an appointment with the visa counselor.

1. Everyone knows that Ms. Gates is a very strict teacher. For one thing, she insists

   that students _____ (*turn in*) their homework on time.

2. In addition, she requires that everyone _____ (*be*) in the

   classroom at 9:00 a.m. sharp.

3. Moreover, whenever she gives a homework assignment, she insists that we

   _____ (*follow*) directions precisely.

4. On the other hand, Ms. Gates is very generous and helpful. For example, if a

   student is having a problem with English, she often recommends that he

   _____ (*study*) a certain section of the book and

   _____ (*discuss*) it with her the next day.

Copyright © 2003 by Pearson Education, Inc.

5. One time I was totally confused about the proper way to use the past perfect

tense. Ms. Gates offered to help me and proposed that I _____

(*meet*) her after school.

B. Combine the pairs of sentences so that the second one becomes a *that*-clause after *It*. Omit the words in parentheses from your new sentence. (*For help, see pages 106–107 of the Handbook.*)

EXAMPLE

This is essential. You (should) see your dentist twice a year.

It is essential that you see your dentist twice a year.

1. This is necessary. You (must) pay your phone bill on time.

_____

2. This is urgent. We (should) call the fire department if we smell gas.

_____

3. This is vital. American workers (must) pay their income taxes by April 15.

_____

4. This is advisable. A person (should) see a doctor if she hits her head.

_____

5. This is important. I (must) buy my textbook before the next class.

_____

Copyright © 2003 by Pearson Education, Inc.

PRACTICE 6

Complete each sentence with the correct form of the verb or verbs in parentheses. Use the base form, infinitive, or past participle. (*For help, see pages 108–109 of the Handbook.*)

EXAMPLE

I have my hair _____*cut*_____ (*cut*) every six weeks.

Laura and Henry were married a week ago. They had a simple, inexpensive, and very beautiful wedding.

1. Laura did not hire a professional dressmaker. Instead, she had her aunt

   _____ (*sew*) her dress.

2. Henry's little nephew wanted to be in the wedding, so they let him

   _____ (*be*) the ring-bearer.

3. Laura and Henry did not need to hire a caterer. Their relatives helped

   _____ (*prepare*) all the food.

4. On the day before the wedding, Laura and Henry bought the flowers

   themselves. Then they had one of Henry's aunts _____

   (*arrange*) them.

5. They got a group of their friends _____ (*decorate*) the

   church.

6. On the day of the wedding, Laura did not get her hair _____

   (*do*). Her sister did it for her.

7. On the afternoon of the wedding, Laura's mother made her

   _____ (*take*) a nap.

8. The couple had Laura's grandfather, a minister, _____

   (*perform*) the marriage ceremony.

Copyright © 2003 by Pearson Education, Inc.

9. Though their friends and relatives helped them _____ (*do*)

almost everything else, Laura and Henry decided to have their wedding

pictures _____ (*take*) by a professional photographer.

10. At the reception, they had the food _____ (*serve*) by

professional waiters because they wanted to let their guests

_____ (*dance*) and _____ (*enjoy*)

themselves.

Copyright © 2003 by Pearson Education, Inc.

PRACTICE I

Edit the following paragraphs for errors in the form of the modals. There are eight mistakes. One sentence has two mistakes, and some sentences have none. The first mistake has been corrected for you as an example. (*For help, see pages 109–111 of the Handbook.*)

Switzerland is a very small country, but it has four official languages: German (70%) , French (20%), Italian (4%), and Romansch (1%). Swiss law states that every school child must ✗ learn at least one second language. As a result, many Swiss people can speaks several languages.

In recent years, English has become increasingly popular in Switzerland. Thousands of tourists visit Switzerland each year, and most of them don't can speak any of the country's official languages. Almost all of them can speaking English, however.

Some Swiss people are worried about the growing use of English in their country. They ask: "What effect will might the use of English have on the relationships between the different linguistic groups in the country?" These people are afraid that English may takes over as the principal method of communication in the country and that this could causing the minor languages to die out. They say that the Swiss people don't must allow this to happen because multilingualism is an essential feature of Swiss history, culture, and identity.

Copyright © 2003 by Pearson Education, Inc.

PRACTICE 2

Complete the following sentences using the appropriate modals. There are several possible answers to some of the sentences. (*For help, see pages 111–117 of the Handbook.*)

EXAMPLE

I left my dictionary at home. _____*May*_____ I borrow yours?

1. Joe likes vegetables better than meat. Therefore, he _____ go to a vegetarian restaurant than a steakhouse.

2. Jennifer gets sunburned easily. Therefore, she _____ wear a hat when she works in the garden.

3. You are in a cafeteria. There are no free tables. At one table, a woman is eating by herself. You approach her and ask, "_____ I please sit here?"

4. If you want to study in the United States, you _____ receive a student visa. You _____ be a U.S. citizen to get a driver's license, however.

5. Your cell phone is not working even though you recharged the battery last night. You conclude, "The battery _____ be defective."

6. Walking down the street, you pass a woman who looks just like your sister. However, your sister is in San Francisco. You say, "That _____ be her."

7. Bella wants to lose weight. Her doctor tells her, "You _____ eat less and exercise more."

Copyright © 2003 by Pearson Education, Inc.

8. In a movie theater, the person in front of you is wearing a tall hat. You say to

   the person, "Excuse me. I _____ see the screen.

   _____ you _____ removing your hat? Thank

   you."

9. A long time ago, girls in U.S. public schools _____ wear skirts

   or dresses. Nowadays they are allowed to wear pants.

PRACTICE 3

Complete the sentences with the perfect form of a modal and the verb in
parentheses. Use one of the following: *could/may/might/should/must/
would/would rather/+ have.* There are several possible answers to some of
the sentences. (*For help, see pages 118–119 of the Handbook.*)

EXAMPLE

Elaine forgot to pay her water bill, so the city turned off her water. She

_____*should have paid*_____ (*pay*) her water bill.

1. Mayumi was late to her English class this morning. She

   _____ (*oversleep*).

2. This morning my car would not start, so I had to find a different way to get to

   work. I _____ (*take*) the bus, but the bus station

   is very far from my house. I _____ (*call*) a taxi,

   but taxis are very expensive. In the end, I called one of my co-workers and

   asked her to give me a ride.

3. My boss is in a very bad mood this morning. He

   _____ (*have*) a fight with his wife.

Copyright © 2003 by Pearson Education, Inc.

4. You had enough money for two pairs of inexpensive shoes or one pair of expensive ones. You bought the inexpensive ones, and they wore out after two months. Looking back, you _____ (*buy*) the expensive ones.

5. Last night Max ate three hamburgers, a large bag of french fries, and a double ice cream cone. Afterward, he felt sick. He _____ (*not eat*) so much.

6. On Friday night, Jenny and her boyfriend went to see a movie. It was terrible. Afterward, both of them agreed that they _____ (*stay*) home.

7. Ching's library book was due yesterday, but she still hasn't returned it. She _____ (*not finish*) reading it yet.

8. Jorge _____ (*not go*) to college without the financial support of his family.

9. I called Steve at 8:00 p.m. last night, but he didn't answer the phone. He _____ (*be*) studying or taking a shower.

10. I _____ (*not make*) that mistake if I had been paying attention.

Copyright © 2003 by Pearson Education, Inc.

PRACTICE I

A. Rewrite the following active sentences as passive sentences. Keep the same verb tense. Use a *by*-phrase only when the performer of the action is known or important. One sentence cannot be changed. (*For help, see pages 120–123 in the Handbook.*)

EXAMPLE

A tornado destroyed many homes.

Many homes were destroyed by a tornado.

1. Every four or five years, we remodel the law office where I work.

2. We are remodeling it now.

3. The office manager hired an interior decorator to plan and manage the work.

4. A crew of workers is doing the physical labor.

5. By the time I arrived this morning, the workers had removed the old carpeting.

6. Painters were painting the manager's office.

7. Someone will deliver the new furniture later this week.

8. They will have finished the whole job by the end of the week.

Copyright © 2003 by Pearson Education, Inc.

9. In the meantime, we have to work with all the dust and noise.

_____

B. Complete the following story with the active or passive form of the verbs in parentheses. (*For help, see pages 120–123 in the Handbook.*)

A two-year-old French poodle (**1**) _____ (*bite*) in

the leg yesterday by a man dressed up as a Siamese cat. The man

(**2**) _____ (*pick up*) by the police after a neighbor

(**3**) _____ (*report*) the incident. The arrested man

(**4**) _____ (*identify*) as Felix Smythe, 36, of Rock Ridge.

Apparently Smythe's Siamese cat (**5**) _____ (*chase, frequently*) by

the French poodle, and Smythe (**6**) _____ (*want*) to get revenge.

Mr. Smythe (**7**) _____ (*charge*) with disturbing the peace, and

the owner of the injured dog (**8**) _____ (*sue*) him now.

PRACTICE 2

A. Rewrite the following paragraph on a separate sheet of paper. Change to the passive voice where possible. Use *by*-phrases where they are appropriate, and omit them when the performer of the action is unknown or unimportant. The first change has been done for you as an example. (*For help, see pages 123–124 of the Handbook.*)

EXAMPLE

Has anyone ever robbed you?

Have you ever been robbed?

_____

Copyright © 2003 by Pearson Education, Inc.

Mr. Paul Jones, a businessman, left his apartment at 7:30 a.m. and returned at 5:00 p.m. As soon as he walked through the door, he could see that someone had robbed his apartment. The robber had taken his computer. He had searched Mr. Jones's closets, and he had dumped all of Mr. Jones's clothes on the floor. A valuable painting was missing. Worst of all, his sweet old cat was dead. Apparently, the robber had poisoned her.

B. Rewrite this paragraph on a separate sheet of paper. Change to the passive voice where possible. Use *by*-phrases where they are appropriate. (*For help, see pages 123–124 of the Handbook.*)

They write the Hebrew alphabet from right to left. They omit vowels in most printed materials. When vowels are used, they place them under the words. The first letter of the Hebrew alphabet is called *alef*. They call the second letter *bet*. This is the origin of the word *alphabet*, which people use in many European languages. Someone invented the Hebrew writing system many thousands of years ago. The Hebrew Bible (which is called the Old Testament by Christians) was written in Hebrew. However, they wrote the New Testament in a language called Aramaic. The common people in Palestine spoke Aramaic at the time of Jesus. Later, someone translated the New Testament from Aramaic into Greek. Most of the translations that are used today are based on the early Greek one.

Copyright © 2003 by Pearson Education, Inc.

PRACTICE I

A. Combine the sentences in each pair. Change the underlined words in the first sentence into a gerund or gerund phrase and make it the subject of the second sentence. Delete the words in parentheses. (*For help, see pages 125–127 of the Handbook.*)

EXAMPLE

(Young people should learn to) manage money. (This) is an important life skill.

Managing money is an important life skill.

1. (Babies love to) play with balls and blocks. (This) helps babies learn how to hold and manipulate objects.

   _____

2. (Young children love to) listen to stories. (This) develops young children's listening and speaking skills.

   _____

3. (Children in kindergarten are taught to) hold a pencil and draw. (This) gets kindergarten children ready for writing.

   _____

B. Form sentences on page 64 with gerund phrases as direct objects. Begin each sentence with *I enjoy* or *I don't enjoy*. Finish the sentence with a gerund phrase made from the words given. (*For help, see pages 125–127 of the Handbook.*)

EXAMPLE

go to the dentist

I don't enjoy going to the dentist.

I enjoy/don't enjoy . . .

1. read the newspaper in the morning

_____

2. see action films

_____

3. play with animals

_____

4. spend time with young children

_____

5. sleep outdoors

_____

C. Complete the sentences by using a gerund or gerund phrase as the direct object. Choose a verb from the list to form each gerund. Use the past form if possible.

clean	copy	study	do	cheat

EXAMPLE

I'm exhausted. I'm going to put off _____*cleaning*_____ the house until

tomorrow.

Yesterday a boy in my class was caught cheating during a test. At first he denied

(1) _____ it, but after the teacher showed him the two nearly

identical test papers, he admitted **(2)** _____ a few answers. The

teacher told him that she would not tolerate **(3)** _____ and gave

him ten extra hours of homework as punishment. She also recommended his

(4) _____ harder in the future.

Copyright © 2003 by Pearson Education, Inc.

PRACTICE 2

Complete the sentences by forming a gerund from the verb in parentheses and adding the correct preposition in front of the gerund. (*For help, see page 128 of the Handbook.*)

EXAMPLE

I plan _____*on meeting*_____ (*meet*) my parents for dinner tonight.

1. When Mrs. Olson had her first child, she left her career as a professional

    singer and devoted herself (**a**) _____ (*raise*) her children.

    Occasionally, during the years when her children were growing up, she would

    dream (**b**) _____ (*sing*) on stage. From time to time, she

    thought (**c**) _____ (*accept*) small singing jobs in the

    community. However, she always decided (**d**) _____ (*take*)

    them because she worried (**e**) _____ (*be*) away from her

    family at night.

2. Professor McNally is a very demanding teacher. He insists

    (**f**) _____ (*give*) his students several hours of homework each

    week. The students often complain (**g**) _____ (*have*) too much

    work, but he does not listen to their complaints. By the end of the semester,

    everyone looks forward (**h**) _____ (*finish*) his course.

3. Last night the people next door had a party. The music was so loud that I

    couldn't concentrate (**i**) _____ (*study*). The laughing and

    talking prevented me (**j**) _____ (*be*) able to focus on my work.

    At midnight I finally went over there and asked them to quiet down. They

    apologized (**k**) _____ (*make*) so much noise.

Copyright © 2003 by Pearson Education, Inc.

PRACTICE 3

Complete the sentences with a preposition and the gerund or base form of the verb or verbs in parentheses. The first item is done for you as an example. (*For help, see page 129 of the Handbook.*)

Last year I graduated from college, got a job, and made the decision to move out of my parents' home. My friends were skeptical about my decision. They thought I was incapable (**1**) _____*of taking*_____ (*take*) care of myself. I had been rather spoiled as a child and was used (**2**) _____ (*have*) everything done for me. However, I was tired (**3**) _____ (*be*) like a child. I was ready to grow up.

Though I was very excited (**4**) _____ (*live*) alone for the first time, I was also concerned (**5**) _____ (*have*) enough money and time to take care of myself. I admit that it was a big adjustment. Living at home, my parents used (**6**) _____ (*do*) everything for me: pay my bills, prepare my food, lend me their car, and so on. As soon as I moved out, I had to get used (**7**) _____ (*do*) all those things for myself. At first it wasn't easy, but I gradually became used (**8**) _____ (*take*) care of myself. I learned how to budget my money and manage my time. I even got accustomed (**9**) _____ (*cook*) for myself.

Now, after a year, I am used (**10**) _____ (*live*) alone, and I really enjoy it. I like being responsible (**11**) _____ (*make*) my own choices. And if I get lonely—well, my family lives just fifteen minutes away.

Copyright © 2003 by Pearson Education, Inc.

PRACTICE 4

A. Choose verbs from the list and write five sentence with *go* + [verb + *ing*] telling when you last did these activities. Write at least five sentences. (*For help, see page 130 of the Handbook.*)

EXAMPLE

swim

I went swimming last August.

bowl	camp	dance	fish	shop	sightsee	swim	ski	hike

1. _____

2. _____

3. _____

4. _____

5. _____

B. Imagine that you are at a crowded outdoor amusement place on a nice afternoon. Complete each of the following sentences with the gerund form of one of the verbs from the list. (*For help, see page 130 of the Handbook.*)

reach	play	blow	take pictures	argue	talk	shine

EXAMPLE

I hear a group of teenagers _____*talking*_____ about pop music.

1. I see some tourists _____.

2. I hear a man and a woman _____ about politics.

Copyright © 2003 by Pearson Education, Inc.

3. I feel the sun _____ and the wind _____

gently on my face.

4. An old woman and her grandson are sitting on a bench. The woman is

listening to the band _____. She doesn't notice her grandson

_____ into her purse and removing her wallet.

C. Complete each sentence with the gerund form of one of the verbs from the list. (*For help, see page 130 of the Handbook.*)

EXAMPLE

A psychology student spent a day _____*observing*_____ children in a

kindergarten class. She sat in the corner and took notes on the things she saw.

play	draw	share	get	open

1. She noticed some children _____ pictures.

2. One child was having difficulty _____ a box of crayons.

3. One child had a hard time _____ the crayons.

4. At one point, the teacher had trouble _____ the children to

be quiet.

5. During recess, everyone had a good time _____ on the

playground.

Copyright © 2003 by Pearson Education, Inc.

PRACTICE I

Complete each sentence with an appropriate infinitive form of the verb in parentheses. Choose from the four forms (present, past, passive, progressive). In some cases, there is more than one correct answer. (*For help, see pages 131–132 of the Handbook.*)

EXAMPLE

Are you planning _____*to go*_____ (*go*) to our school reunion

next month?

1. It was kind of him _____ (*carry*) that heavy box for me.

2. This check needs _____ (*sign*) before it can be deposited in

the bank.

3. Stop watching television. You need _____ (*study*) for your

history test tomorrow.

4. Can you teach me how _____ (*tune*) a guitar?

5. Research shows that newborn babies need _____ (*pick up*)

and _____ (*hold*) in order to develop normally.

6. I am very pleased _____ (*meet*) you, Mr. President.

7. The last time I saw my nephew, he appeared _____ (*grow*) at

least ten centimeters.

8. I hope _____ (*live*) in my own apartment by this time next

year.

9. It is extremely dangerous _____ (*drive*) a car if you have

been drinking alcohol.

10. Jack is an outstanding worker. He deserves _____ (*promote*).

Copyright © 2003 by Pearson Education, Inc.

PRACTICE 2

Rewrite each sentence with *it* and an infinitive phrase. Add the noun or pronoun in parentheses (if one is given) and an appropriate preposition (*for, of,* or *to*) in front of the infinitive phrase. (*For help, see pages 132–133 of the Handbook.*)

EXAMPLE

Learning about local customs in different countries is very important. (*travelers*)

It is very important for travelers to learn about local customs in different countries.

1. Removing shoes is courteous when entering a Japanese home. (*people*)

2. In many countries, making noises while eating is polite because it shows that the food is tasty. (*guests*)

3. In the United States, pointing at someone with your middle finger is very rude.

4. Tasting new foods was fascinating when I visited Indonesia. (*me*)

Copyright © 2003 by Pearson Education, Inc.

5. Calling teachers by their first names often feels strange. (*students who come to study in the United States*)

_____

_____

6. Making eye contact is necessary in some cultures. (*speakers*)

_____

_____

7. In other cultures, avoiding eye contact as a way of showing respect is preferable.

_____

_____

8. Learning that in some cultures white is the color of death was surprising. (*me*)

_____

_____

9. Offering a bribe to a police officer is foolish in North America. (*drivers*)

_____

_____

10. Asking questions is useful when you are in a new place.

_____

_____

Copyright © 2003 by Pearson Education, Inc.

PRACTICE 3

Complete each sentence with an infinitive phrase from the box. Add a noun or pronoun after the verb if necessary. There are many possible answers. (*For help, see pages 134–135 of the Handbook.*)

do their best	develop their talents
think for themselves	pursue their dreams
accept laziness	do their own work
be responsible adults	not copy
praise students' efforts	ask questions
find their own answers	solve their own problems
be independent thinkers	work effectively in groups

What do excellent teachers do?

EXAMPLE

They teach *students to use their time wisely.* _____

1. They motivate _____

2. They challenge _____

3. They never fail _____

4. They allow _____

5. They refuse _____

6. They help _____

7. They encourage _____

8. They expect _____

9. They show _____ how _____

10. They urge _____

Copyright © 2003 by Pearson Education, Inc.

PRACTICE 4

A. Use these infinitive phrases to write questions and answers about superstitions. Your answers should be truthful. Follow the example. (*For help, see page 136 of the Handbook.*)

EXAMPLE

Would you feel lucky / find a coin on the sidewalk

Q: *Would you feel lucky to find a coin on the sidewalk?*

A: *Yes, I would feel lucky to find a coin on the sidewalk.* OR

No, I would not feel lucky to find a coin on the sidewalk.

1. Would you feel lucky / find a four-leaf clover

Q: _____

A: _____

2. Would you feel horrified / break a mirror

Q: _____

A: _____

3. Would you be afraid / go out on Friday the thirteenth

Q: _____

A: _____

4. Would you feel fortunate / see a shooting star

Q: _____

A: _____

5. Would you be careful / not walk under a ladder

Q: _____

A: _____

Copyright © 2003 by Pearson Education, Inc.

B. Use infinitive phrases to form sentences about early "firsts" in aviation. Follow the example. (*For help, see page 136 of the Handbook.*)

EXAMPLE

1910: Baroness Raymonde de la Roche of France—woman—receive a pilot's license

In 1910, Baroness Raymonde de la Roche of France was the first woman to

receive a pilot's license.

1. 1926: Floyd Bennet and Robert Byrd—people—fly over the North Pole

_____

_____

2. 1927: Charles Lindbergh—person—fly nonstop across the Atlantic Ocean alone

_____

_____

3. 1932: Amelia Earhart—woman—repeat Lindbergh's accomplishment

_____

_____

C. Use infinitive phrases with the passive voice to form sentences about "hi-tech" houses. (*For help, see page 136 of the Handbook.*)

EXAMPLE

timers / turn lights on and off

Timers can be used to turn lights on and off.

Copyright © 2003 by Pearson Education, Inc.

1. computers / order groceries

   _____

2. electric mixers / prepare cakes

   _____

3. microwave ovens / cook meals

   _____

4. robots / vacuum the house

   _____

PRACTICE 5

A. Complete each sentence with *very, too,* or *enough* and the word in parentheses. (*For help, see pages 137–138 of the Handbook.*)

EXAMPLE

Do you think a 12-year-old is __*responsible enough*__ (*responsible*) to babysit?

Sarah, a 14-year-old girl, is having an argument with her mother.

SARAH: Robbie invited me to go to a party with him on Saturday night.

MOTHER: Alone? No, Sarah. You are (**1**) _____ (*young*) to go

out alone with boys.

SARAH: Please, Mom! You always say that I am (**2**) _____

(*mature*) for my age. If I'm (**3**) _____ (*old*) to babysit

and stay home by myself, how come I'm not (**4**) _____

(*old*) to go out with boys?

Copyright © 2003 by Pearson Education, Inc.

MOTHER: I agree that you are (**5**) _____ (*responsible*) in some

ways. However, you are not (**6**) _____ (*experienced*)

to go out on dates yet.

SARAH: How can I get experience if you won't let me go?

MOTHER: Be patient, Sarah. I know it's (**7**) _____ (*hard*) to wait,

but until you're sixteen, you can keep going out with your friends in

groups.

B. Read each situation. Then complete the sentence with *too* or *enough*, an adjective or a noun, and an infinitive that completes the meaning. (*For help, see pages 137–138 of the Handbook.*)

EXAMPLE

He lives far away. He can't walk to school.

He lives *too far away to walk to school.* _____

Jean is worried because her 85-year-old grandfather is still driving.

1. His eyes are weak. He can't see the traffic signs.

His eyes are _____

2. His hearing isn't good. He can't hear emergency vehicles.

His hearing isn't _____

3. His reflexes aren't quick. He can't react quickly.

His reflexes are _____

4. However, he is very stubborn. He won't give up driving.

He is _____

Copyright © 2003 by Pearson Education, Inc.

Complete each sentence with the gerund or infinitive form of the verb in parentheses. In some cases both are correct. (*For help, see pages 139–140 of the Handbook.*)

EXAMPLE

I love ___to travel / traveling___ (*travel*).

1. However, I hate _____ (*pack*) my suitcases. I always worry

   that I will forget _____ (*pack*) something important.

2. I always arrive at the airport early because I can't stand

   _____ (*wait*) in lines.

3. When I travel, I always try _____ (*talk*) to the local residents.

4. I prefer _____ (*stay*) in small pensions or bed-and-breakfasts

   instead of large, impersonal hotels.

5. Before I get off an airplane, I always stop _____ (*check*)

   whether I have left anything behind.

6. Last year I took a trip to Turkey. While I was planning my trip, a Turkish

   friend advised me _____ (*check*) the Internet for good deals

   on hotels.

7. I found out that the Turkish government does not permit tourists

   _____ (*enter*) the country without a visa.

8. My friend told me that Turkey has many beautiful old mosques, and if I went

   inside them, I must remember _____ (*take off*) my shoes.

9. "When you shop in Turkey, you should always attempt

   _____ (*bargain*) with the shopkeepers," she said. "Don't pay

   the first price they ask."

Copyright © 2003 by Pearson Education, Inc.   **77**

10. Before I departed for my vacation, I remembered _____ (*get*) some Turkish money.

11. After two weeks, it was already time for me to return home. I regretted not _____ (*be*) able to stay longer.

12. My trip to Turkey was like a wonderful dream. After I returned from my vacation, I couldn't stop _____ (*think*) about it.

Copyright © 2003 by Pearson Education, Inc.

12d   Phrasal verbs

Complete the following sentences with phrasal verbs from the box below. Some verbs are separable. You will use all the items. (*For help, see page 141 of the Handbook.*)

throw out / throw away	pass away	show up
	take back	drop in
keep on	take off	dress up
get together		
	try on	stand up
stay up		

1. In many cultures, it is customary for a man to _____ his hat

   when he comes indoors. Religious Jewish men, in contrast,

   _____ their hats _____ all the time,

   even indoors.

2. In the United States, people used to _____ to go to cultural

   events such as concerts or operas. These days, many people wear casual clothes

   on these occasions.

3. In the Philippines, people believe it is bad luck for a bride to

   _____ her wedding dress _____ before

   the wedding.

4. In many cultures, it is common for friends and relatives to

   _____ on each other frequently. In the United States, however,

   it is customary to call before you visit somebody.

5. To prepare for the coming New Year, people in many cultures clean their

   homes and _____ anything old, broken, or useless. They

_____ until midnight on New Year's Eve. On New Year's Day,

families _____ and eat traditional foods.

6. In many small, rural places, it is traditional for everyone in town to come to

   weddings and other happy occasions. In large cities, though, it is rude to

   _____ without a formal invitation.

7. In most cultures, it is polite for young people to _____ when

   an older person enters the room.

8. In some cultures, it is customary to have a party when a beloved person

   _____.

9. In the United States, if you purchase something and later decide you don't like

   it, you may _____ the item _____ to the

   store as long as you have a receipt.

Copyright © 2003 by Pearson Education, Inc.

Choose the correct form of the verb by circling it. (*For help, see pages 142–148 of the Handbook.*)

EXAMPLE

Each of the children (has)/ have a pencil and a notebook.

1. Both of my parents <u>was / were</u> born in Germany.

2. Bread and butter <u>is / are</u> always served at the beginning of the meal.

3. Each piece of candy in the box <u>is / are</u> wrapped separately.

4. None of the managers <u>is / are</u> in the office at the moment.

5. One-half of the students in Ms. Baker's class <u>speak / speaks</u> Spanish.

6. Either Mr. or Mrs. Johnson always <u>stay / stays</u> home with the children.

7. The firefighters <u>is / are</u> responding to the emergency.

8. Every dish at that restaurant <u>is / are</u> a culinary masterpiece.

9. Most of the people in our small town <u>make / makes</u> a living from farming.

10. There <u>is / are</u> several mistakes in the letter you wrote.

11. The principal export crop of the country <u>is / are</u> bananas.

12. Physics <u>is / are</u> the most difficult course I am taking.

13. The staff <u>is / are</u> planning a surprise party for the president of the company.

14. Sheep <u>is / are</u> raised in Ireland.

15. Neither the Toyota nor the Honda <u>come / comes</u> with a built-in phone.

16. Doctors who <u>work / works</u> exclusively with children <u>is / are</u> called pediatricians.

17. <u>Is / Are</u> there any more milk in the carton?

18. The noise from cars passing by my house <u>make / makes</u> it hard for me to concentrate.

19. Hair <u>grows / grow</u> at the rate of approximately half an inch per month.

Copyright © 2003 by Pearson Education, Inc.

Which underlined part of each sentence is correct? Cross out the incorrect part. (*For help, see pages 149–152 of the Handbook.*)

EXAMPLE

My favorite sweater is made of wool/~~a wool~~ and cotton/~~a cotton~~.

It's Saturday morning.

WIFE: I wish I didn't have to go to (**1**) work/a work today. I'd like to stay

home, light (**2**) fire/a fire in the fireplace, and read all day. Anyway,

what are you going to do today?

HUSBAND: Oh, you know. First there's (**3**) a stuff/some stuff I want to do

around the house. I'll go through (**4**) some mail/a mail and clean out

(**5**) some junk/a junk from the garage. It's time to get rid of

(**6**) some garbage/a garbage out there! If I have (**7**) time/a time, I'll

watch (**8**) some soccer/a soccer on (**9**) television/a television.

WIFE: Could you go to the supermarket? We're pretty low on

(**10**) a food/food.

HUSBAND: Sure, no problem. What do we need?

WIFE: (**11**) Coffee/A coffee, (**12**) milk/a milk, (**13**) some ice cream/an ice

cream, (**14**) some lettuce/a lettuce . . . oh, and we're out of

(**15**) mayonnaise/a mayonnaise.

HUSBAND: What about (**16**) dinner/a dinner? Do you want to eat at home

tonight or go out?

WIFE: Let's eat at home. I'm in the mood for (**17**) chicken/a chicken with

that wonderful garlic sauce you make. Would you mind making it?

    Copyright © 2003 by Pearson Education, Inc.

HUSBAND: OK, I can do that. I'll get (**18**) <u>a spinach / some spinach</u> and

potatoes to go with it, and we can have (**19**) <u>cheese / a cheese</u> and

(**20**) <u>fruit / a fruit</u> for dessert.

WIFE: That sounds delicious. Oh, and one more thing. We need

(**21**) <u>luggage / a luggage</u> for our next vacation. Would you mind

going to the mall and seeing what they have?

HUSBAND: No problem, boss. Is there anything else?

Copyright © 2003 by Pearson Education, Inc.

Cross out all the expressions that cannot complete the sentences. The first one is done as an example. (*For help, see pages 152–155 of the Handbook.*)

Recently I took up a new hobby: gardening. I began by reading (~~one~~, *a couple of, a few, ~~a little~~*) books about it, and I talked to (*a number of, few of, some of*) my friends who are experienced gardeners. I don't have (*much, many, a lot of, some*) spare time, so my friends recommended (*every, a little, a few, any*) plants that would look nice and wouldn't require (*much, many, several, a little*) care.

After that, I paid my first visit to a gardening store. I spent (*both, a couple of, a number of, any*) hours talking to the workers and looking at plants. There were (*much, many, few, a lot of*) varieties, and I had a difficult time choosing what to buy. I wish I could have bought (*every, each, both, all*) plant in the store! In the end, though, I selected (*a couple of, a number of, a great deal of, a few*) small bushes, (*several, a little, every, five*) types of flowers, and (*some, several, much, a great deal of*) packages of vegetable seeds. I also bought (*some, one, a few, many*) tools and (*a lot of, a great deal of, much, many*) fertilizer because the earth in my garden is not very rich.

It took me a couple of weeks to plant everything. Now, (*several, a few, both, much*) months later, the plants are blooming and the vegetables are growing. It doesn't require (*much, many, a lot of, plenty of*) effort to keep the garden going. I spend (*an, a few, several, some*) hours working there (*each, every, several, all*) weekend and I make sure to give the plants (*lots of, plenty of, much, most*) water. I get (*a great deal of, plenty of, lots of, a couple of*) pleasure from my beautiful garden.

   Copyright © 2003 by Pearson Education, Inc.

Write *G* (generic) in the blank spaces in front of generic nouns. Write *NG* (not generic) in front of concrete nouns. (*For help, see page 157 of the Handbook.*)

EXAMPLE

I love __*G*__ coffee, and __*NG*__ French-roast coffee is my absolute favorite.

1. _____ Lions are wild animals, but _____ the lions at the local zoo seem quite tame.

2. Is _____ a tomato a fruit or a vegetable?

3. Since the 1920s, _____ cars have been made mainly of steel. Nowadays, however, more and more car parts are made of plastic. The DaimlerChrysler company, for example, is planning to manufacture _____ a car body made entirely of plastic.

4. _____ A drunk driver hit my car while I was stopped for a red light. Fortunately, I was not hurt, but unfortunately, he did not have _____ car insurance.

5. I don't usually like _____ dogs, but _____ my neighbor's dog is an exception.

6. _____ The telephone was invented by Alexander Graham Bell.

7. My daughter has asked for _____ a telephone for her twelfth birthday.

8. The wedding invitations were printed on _____ cream-colored paper.

Cross out the incorrect article in each pair. (*For help, see pages 159–161 of the Handbook.*)

EXAMPLE

I work for a/~~the~~ car manufacturer, and I travel a great deal on business.

Last week, I had (**1**) <u>an</u>/the amusing experience. There were (**2**) the/<u>some</u> professional basketball players on my flight to Chicago. (**3**) <u>The</u>/Some players were all young, lean, and tall. (**4**) A/<u>The</u> tallest was nearly 7 feet; (**5**) <u>a</u>/the shortest was at least 6 feet 2. I am only 5 feet 8, and (**6**) an/<u>the</u> amusing thing was that I was assigned (**7**) <u>a</u>/the seat on (**8**) <u>a</u>/the aisle, while two of the players had (**9**) <u>a</u>/the middle and window seats next to me. Unfortunately (**10**) <u>a</u>/the plane was full, so there were no empty aisle seats for them to move to. Feeling sorry for them, I offered to exchange seats with one of them. But which one? Both of them were equally uncomfortable. They discussed (**11**) <u>a</u>/the matter and decided that (**12**) <u>a</u>/the only fair solution was to flip (**13**) <u>a</u>/the coin. They did it, and (**14**) <u>a</u>/the player next to (**15**) <u>a</u>/the window lost. His friend moved to (**16**) <u>an</u>/the aisle, I sat in (**17**) <u>a</u>/the middle, and he spent most of (**18**) <u>a</u>/the flight to Chicago standing and walking around (**19**) <u>a</u>/the plane.

Copyright © 2003 by Pearson Education, Inc.

Complete the paragraphs with appropriate articles. Sometimes no article is necessary (Ø). (*For help, see pages 156–164 of the Handbook.*)

EXAMPLE

We took _____*a*_____ vacation in _____*the*_____ the national parks of _____*Ø*_____

Alberta, _____*Ø*_____ Canada.

A. We learn in (1) _____ geography courses that (2) _____ valley

surrounding (3) _____ Nile River in (4) _____ Egypt is one of

(5) _____ most fertile places in (6) _____ world. Each year

(7) _____ river floods, bringing (8) _____ minerals to the soil. In

ancient times, (9) _____ fertility of this region attracted many people. As

a result, (10) _____ Egypt became (11) _____ first known civilized

country. It is often referred to as "(12) _____ Cradle of Civilization."

B. (1) _____ Library of Congress, (2) _____ national library of

(3) _____ United States, is located near (4) _____ Capitol building

in (5) _____ Washington, D.C. (6) _____ main purpose of

(7) _____ library is to serve (8) _____ members of Congress, but it

is also open to (9) _____ public as (10) _____ reference library.

(11) _____ library contains (12) _____ copy of every book

published in (13) _____ United States. There are also collections of

(14) _____ musical instruments, recordings, maps, photographs,

and documents. One of (15) _____ most famous documents in

(16) _____ library is (17) _____ first draft of (18) _____

speech by Abraham Lincoln.

C. You do not need (**1**) _____ car to get around in (**2**) _____

New York City. The five boroughs[1] of (**3**) _____ city are connected by

(**4**) _____ extensive system of (**5**) _____ subways and trains. In

(**6**) _____ Manhattan, people get around either on (**7**) _____ foot

or by (**8**) _____ taxi. Very few people drive there because (**9**) _____

parking is both expensive and scarce.

---

[1]**boroughs:** geographical areas within a city

Copyright © 2003 by Pearson Education, Inc.

A. Complete the sentences with appropriate pronouns. (*For help, see pages 165–167 of the Handbook.*)

EXAMPLE

Bill Gates, the chairman of Microsoft Corporation, was born on October 28, 1955, and grew up in Seattle, Washington, with _____*his*_____ two sisters.

1. Gates, _____ mother was a schoolteacher, attended public elementary school. He was a skinny, shy, awkward boy _____ had exceptional talent in math and logic. Gates wrote _____ first computer program at age thirteen.

2. Gates entered Harvard University in 1973 but dropped out in 1975 when _____ and Paul Allen, a childhood friend of _____ , founded Microsoft. Guided by the vision that every home and office would one day have a computer, _____ began developing software for personal computers.

3. Microsoft became a publicly owned company in 1986. The following year, the company introduced _____ first version of Windows, _____ became the most popular operating system in the world. Gates became one of the richest men in the world.

4. Melinda French, _____ Gates married in 1994, had been a marketing executive at Microsoft. With _____ , Gates established a charitable foundation. Until now, _____ have given away more than $24 billion to organizations working on global health and education.

Copyright © 2003 by Pearson Education, Inc.

B. Circle the correct pronoun. (*For help, see pages 165–167 of the Handbook.*)

1. My friend Joyce is more comfortable with computers than I/me.

2. However, I am a better writer than she/her.

3. Joyce and I/me decided to put our talents together and start an Internet

business.

4. We asked Beth, another friend who/whom we had gone to school with, to be

our business manager.

5. Beth, whose/who her major had been accounting, agreed to join us.

6. To start our business, we borrowed $50,000 from an uncle of me/mine/my

who/whom had been a very successful businessman before retiring at

the age of 55.

7. We hope our/ours company will start making a profit within two years.

Copyright © 2003 by Pearson Education, Inc.

A. Add an appropriate reflexive pronoun to the following sentences. (*For help, see pages 168–169 of the Handbook.*)

EXAMPLE

My cat, Annabelle, spends hours each day licking _____*herself*_____.

1. **A:** What happened to you? Your face is bleeding.

   B: It's nothing. I cut _____ shaving.

2. At what age will you allow your son to stay home by _____?

3. Linda and Tom cannot afford to hire a gardener, so they take care of their

   garden _____.

4. Do you like my hair? I cut it _____.

5. Our English class is going to have a Halloween party next week. The students

   _____ will decorate the room and make all the food.

B. Find and correct four pronoun errors in the following passage. (*For help, see pages 168–169 of the Handbook.*)

When I was a child, both my parents worked outside the house, so my four

brothers and sisters and I sometimes stayed home by ourself. It was not a problem

for us to be alone because the older ones took care of the younger ones, and we all

knew we could depend on each another. Our parents always encouraged us to be

independent. As a result, from a young age, I learned to solve problems by

mineself. Today I am a father too, and I also encourage my children to do as many

things as possible for theirselves.

Copyright © 2003 by Pearson Education, Inc.

Revise the following passages to correct nine errors in pronoun agreement. The first mistake has been corrected for you as an example. (*For help, see pages 170–172 of the Handbook.*)

1. Security arrangements at airports have become very strict. Now, departing passengers are required to come to the airport three hours before ~~his~~ *their* flight. Upon arrival, each passenger is required to have their luggage checked. If someone is carrying a gun or any kind of sharp object, they will be questioned and possibly even arrested.

2. Passengers must pass through a metal detector and have their carry-on bags x-rayed. At this point, they must say good-bye to their family and friends because no one except passengers with tickets are allowed past the metal detectors.

3. Procedures for picking up arriving passengers have also changed. In the past, passengers could be met at the gate as soon as he or she got off the plane. Nowadays, he must be met in the baggage-claim area.

4. Last week my parents and my brother flew to London together. The security check before the flight took more than an hour. Luckily, neither my brother nor my parents were told to open his bags.

5. The new security measures are time-consuming and inconvenient. Nevertheless, most people cooperate with it because everybody understands that these measures could save their life.

Copyright © 2003 by Pearson Education, Inc.

Revise each passage to correct errors in pronoun reference. The number of corrections you need to make is given in parentheses. The first error is corrected for you as an example. (*For help, see page 173 of the Handbook.*)

1. (4 corrections) Academic dishonesty, or cheating, is a rising problem on

   university campuses. My college recently announced strict new measures for

   dealing with ~~this~~ *this problem*. According to the new rules, any student caught cheating will

   fail the course in which the cheating occurred. If it happens again, the student

   will be expelled from the university. Many students were upset about that. They

   said that it wasn't fair because under the new rules, a student's entire career

   could be destroyed by one "mistake."

2. (4 corrections) My roommate was one of the first people punished under the

   new rules. His physics professor caught him cheating during a test. He saw him

   looking at notes he had hidden in his sleeve. Because it was his first offense, he

   got an F, and he will have to repeat it in summer school. When I asked him

   why he had cheated instead of studying a little harder, his excuse was

   "Everyone does it."

Copyright © 2003 by Pearson Education, Inc.

Edit the conversation for nine errors in the position of adjectives and adverbs.
(*For help, see pages 174–176 of the Handbook.*)

EXAMPLE

I put ⌒(each night) my glasses on a table next to my bed.

A husband and wife are expecting his parents for dinner. They are preparing the meal in the kitchen.

WIFE: Well, dinner is ready almost.

HUSBAND: What can I do to help? Do you want me to make the salad?

WIFE: I made this morning the salad. Let's see. . . . We're having soup

chicken. I made it last night, so we need to heat it. Could you take it

out of the refrigerator and put it on the stove? Lift carefully the pot;

it's heavy.

HUSBAND: OK. What else?

WIFE: Check the table. I can't remember if I put out soup spoons.

HUSBAND: Already I've done it.

An hour later.

WIFE: I'm getting worried about your parents. They're late half an hour. It's

time the first they've been late ever. Why haven't they called us?

HUSBAND: I don't know. They're stuck in traffic probably. But if they don't arrive

soon, I'm going to call the police.

                                      Copyright © 2003 by Pearson Education, Inc.

Edit the sentences for ten errors in word order and comma use. Some sentences have no errors. (*For help, see pages 177–178 of the Handbook.*)

My family originates from Greece, so when my cousin got married last week, she had a Greek Orthodox church traditional ceremony. She wore a silk old-fashioned cream gown with a lace long train, and she carried a bouquet of red, yellow, and white flowers. The groom, who also comes from a Greek family very large, wore a gray formal suit.

The afternoon wedding was followed by a very loud, festive party in the evening. The guests talked, laughed, sang, danced, and ate huge quantities of Greek delicious food. There was a band fantastic that played music both traditional and modern. I loved seeing my old tiny grandmother dancing with the slightly embarrassed groom.

My cousin received many wonderful wedding gifts. However, she told me that her favorite gift was a pair of silver antique candlesticks that she got from our grandmother.

Copyright © 2003 by Pearson Education, Inc.

Complete each sentence with the correct participial adjective of the verb in parentheses. (*For help, see page 178 of the Handbook.*)

EXAMPLE

I rarely watch television because I think most programs are

_____*boring*_____ (*bore*).

1. James was very _____ (*embarrass*) when he was unable to

   remember the name of his boss's wife.

2. I enjoy working in the garden for two reasons. First, it is very

   _____ (*relax*) to dig in the earth and spend time among

   plants. In addition, it is very _____ (*satisfy*) to plant flowers

   and watch them grow.

3. **A:** Do you like roller coasters?

   B: No! They're _____ (*terrify*)! Last summer I went to

   Six Flags with my boyfriend, and we rode on the biggest roller coaster

   in the park. I was so _____ (*frighten*), I thought I

   was going to faint. But my boyfriend loved it. He thought it was so

   _____ (*thrill*) that he wanted to go again. I said, "Fine,

   go ahead—but without me!"

4. **A:** Do you think it's possible for animals to feel _____

   (*depress*)?

   B: Sure. My dog always gets really quiet when he sees me packing a suitcase.

   He knows I'm going away, and he has no way of knowing that I'm coming

   back. I'm sure it must be very _____ (*confuse*) for him.

   Copyright © 2003 by Pearson Education, Inc.

5. **WOMAN:** Do you know what bothers me?

   FRIEND: What?

   WOMAN: When my husband leaves his towel on the bathroom floor instead of

   hanging it up. It is so _____ (*irritate*)!

6. I read a story in the newspaper about three hikers who were lost in the

   mountains for three days without food or shelter. When they were finally

   rescued, they were _____ (*exhaust*).

Copyright © 2003 by Pearson Education, Inc.

In the following passage, write the correct forms of the words in parentheses. The symbols indicate a degree of comparison: + means "greater," – means "smaller," and = means "equal." Add necessary words such as *more/less, most/least, than, the.* (*For help, see pages 179–183 of the Handbook.*)

Three popular family cars—the Volkswagen Passat, the Honda Accord, and the Ford Taurus—were evaluated and compared by an independent car-testing company. Following is a summary of the test results.[1]

The car that got (**1**) _____ *the highest* _____ (+ *high*) overall

evaluation was the Passat. It had (**2**) _____

(+ *smooth*) ride, it was (**3**) _____ (– *noisy*), and

evaluators said it was by far (**4**) _____ (+ *enjoyable*)

to drive. The Passat was also slightly (**5**) _____

(+ *roomy*) the Honda and the Taurus, but it was

(**6**) _____ (+ *expensive*) of the three cars.

The Honda Accord, which was ranked second, received almost

(**7**) _____ (= *many points*) the Passat. The

two cars were similar in many ways. For example, the Honda was

(**8**) _____ (= *comfortable*) and

(**9**) _____ (= *safe*) the Passat. However, in two

categories, the Honda was superior: It got (**10**) _____

(+ *good gas mileage*), and it was much (**11**) _____

(– *expensive*).

---

[1]*Source:* Edmunds.com.
http://www.edmunds.com/reviews/comparison/articles/43901/article.html

                    Copyright © 2003 by Pearson Education, Inc.

The Taurus, which came in third, had nearly

(**12**) _____ (= *number of optional features*)

_____ the Honda. It was

(**13**) _____ (+ *quiet*) the Accord though not

(**14**) _____ (= *quiet*) the Passat. However, according

to the testers, it was much (**15**) _____ (– *comfortable*)

the other two cars. While it was considered to be

(**16**) _____ (– *attractive*) of the three cars, it was also

(**17**) _____ (– *expensive*). Nevertheless, in recent

years, the Taurus has not sold sell (**18**) _____ (= *well*)

the Honda Accord. In fact, the Accord is (**19**) _____

(+ *popular*) car of its size in the United States.

Copyright © 2003 by Pearson Education, Inc.

Edit the following sentences for errors in the use of negative words. Two sentences have two errors. (*For help, see pages 185–186 of the Handbook.*)

EXAMPLE

> *any*
> There weren't ~~no~~ ripe bananas at the market this morning.

Mr. Connolly recently started a new job.

1. Now he makes a lot of money, but he is no happy.

2. He has to leave the house at 6:30 a.m., so he is no home when his children wake up in the morning.

3. He no come home until 7:00 or 8:00 in the evening.

4. He no can eat dinner with his family.

5. He don't barely has time to see his children before they go to bed.

6. In the evenings, he has not energy to do nothing except watch television.

7. His wife complains, "You don't never talk to me no more."

8. Mr. Connolly regrets taking the new job. It's nice to have more money, but after all, money is no everything.

Copyright © 2003 by Pearson Education, Inc.

A. Edit the following sentences for errors in the use of adjective clauses. (*For help, see pages 186–191 of the Handbook.*)

EXAMPLE

         whom

I apologized to the woman ~~who~~ I spilled coffee on ~~her~~.

1. There is something I want to say it to you, so listen carefully.

2. My father's mother, who her house is near the beach, swims in the ocean every day.

3. In Chinatown, there are thousands of Chinese people who doesn't speak English.

4. I have a very strange neighbor who she lives by herself and never talks to anybody.

5. Our teacher told us a hilarious story, who has a wonderful sense of humor.

6. W. A. Mozart was born in Salzburg, Austria. Which was a famous center for music.

B. Combine the sentences in each pair on page 102 to make one sentence. Change the second sentence in each pair to an adjective clause. (*For help, see pages 186–191 of the Handbook.*)

EXAMPLE

Did you buy the dress? You looked at it yesterday.

Did you buy the dress that / which / Ø you looked at yesterday?

Copyright © 2003 by Pearson Education, Inc.

1. The students raised their hands. Their names were called.

   _____

2. The girl was very helpful. She explained the homework to me.

   _____

3. On our trip, we visited many areas of the United States. We had never seen them before.

   _____

4. The place is a secret. We are taking you to that place.

   _____

5. The woman stepped on my toe. I was dancing with her.

   _____

6. Early morning is the time. I do my best work then.

   _____

7. The student is in one of my classes. You just met her parents.

   _____

Copyright © 2003 by Pearson Education, Inc.

24 End Punctuation

Add or substitute periods, question marks, and exclamation points. (*For help, see pages 194–195 in the Handbook.*)

EXAMPLE

Last Saturday was my thirtieth birthday⊙

1. My husband said he wanted to take me out to dinner!

2. He asked me which restaurant I wanted to go to?

3. I thought about it for a while

4. What kind of food did I feel like having Mexican French Indian Persian

5. Finally I chose a French restaurant that some friends had recommended

6. My husband made a reservation for 7:00 p m

7. However, without my knowledge, he made some other plans as well!

8. When we arrived at the restaurant, we were escorted to a private room

9. As we walked in, I saw about fifteen of our friends sitting there

10. "Surprise" they shouted

Copyright © 2003 by Pearson Education, Inc.

Edit the following sentences for the correct use of commas. One sentence is correct. Two sentences have two mistakes. (*For help, see pages 196–197 of the Handbook.*)

EXAMPLE

I live in an apartment/in downtown Chicago.

1. Living downtown has both advantages, and disadvantages.

2. My office is downtown so I can walk to work most of the time.

3. I enjoy being close to theaters, and museums.

4. Shopping is very convenient and there are many excellent restaurants nearby.

5. On the other hand, I don't like the traffic, or the noise of the big city.

6. My friends complain, that it is difficult to find parking near my apartment.

7. My family does not live near me so I sometimes feel isolated, and lonely.

8. Now I am single so I think the advantages of living downtown, are greater than the disadvantages.

9. If I get married someday, I hope to buy a house in the suburbs and plant a garden.

     Copyright © 2003 by Pearson Education, Inc.

25b Commas after introducers

Edit the following sentences for the correct use of commas. Three sentences are correct. The first error is corrected for you as an example. (*For help, see pages 198–199 of the Handbook.*)

Ms. Baker is an English teacher. This is the way she prepares her lessons.

1. To begin, she sits at her desk and thinks about what she needs to teach the next day.

2. Soon she decides that she needs a cup of coffee.

3. She goes to the kitchen, puts the water on the stove to boil, and returns to her desk.

4. Then she opens her books and starts to plan the lessons.

5. Almost immediately she stops working and starts to daydream about the party on Saturday night.

6. Another interruption, comes when the phone rings.

7. While she is talking on the phone the water on the stove boils.

8. As quickly as possible she ends the conversation, goes to the kitchen, and prepares the coffee.

9. Carrying the cup of coffee she returns to her desk once again.

10. Before long she looks at the clock and realizes it is time to watch her favorite program on television.

11. In the end Ms. Baker decides that the lessons will have to wait until later.

Copyright © 2003 by Pearson Education, Inc.

A. Insert one or more commas in one of the sentences in each pair. (*For help, see pages 199–201 of the Handbook.*)

EXAMPLE

a: The lamp which I bought at a garage sale is more than one hundred years old.

b: That blue lamp, which I bought at a garage sale, is more than one hundred years old.

1. **a:** The man who lives next door has six daughters.

   b: Mr. Jones who lives next door has six daughters.

2. **a:** Our town's biggest law firm recently hired a new lawyer. The lawyer who went to Harvard Law School will no doubt receive an excellent salary.

   b: A lawyer who graduated from Harvard Law School will no doubt receive an excellent salary.

3. **a:** A young woman running to board the train slipped on the platform, fell, and broke her arm.

   b: My secretary running to board the train slipped on the platform, fell, and broke her arm.

4. **a:** The president of the United States has two homes. The primary residence located in Washington, D.C. is the White House.

   b: The residence located near Thurmont, Maryland, is known as Camp David.

Copyright © 2003 by Pearson Education, Inc.

5. a: Strawberries which grow in warm weather are not available during the winter.

   b: Fruit which grows in warm weather is not available during the winter.

6. a: My sister Joyce lives in San Diego. (*I have one sister.*)

   b: My sister Joyce lives in San Diego. (*I have two sisters.*)

B. Add or delete commas as needed in the following sentences. (*For help, see pages 199–201 of the Handbook.*)

1. My oldest brother Kenneth is married to my wife's sister.

2. Children, learning to speak two languages at the same time, do not mix languages very often.

3. Many countries, that have a king or a queen, also have a prime minister or president.

4. Vitamin D which aids in bone and tooth formation can be toxic in very large amounts.

5. After winning $50,000 in the lottery, my uncle bought a beautiful house, located on the shore of a lake.

Copyright © 2003 by Pearson Education, Inc.

Edit the following passages for the correct use of commas. There are **nine** errors. The first correction is done for you as an example. (*For help, see page 202 of the Handbook.*)

1. Do you know the difference between an alligator and a crocodile? One difference can be seen in the animal's nose, or snout. An alligator has a wide, round snout. The snout of a crocodile, in contrast, is longer and more pointed.

2. Alligators are found in only two places in the world: the United States and China. In the United States, the wild alligator population is estimated to number more than 1 million animals. On the other hand the Chinese alligator, which is smaller than its American cousin, is nearly extinct.

3. There are many myths about alligators. For example many people believe that they can live for hundreds of years. This is untrue however; in fact wild alligators live to be 30 or 40 years old, while captive alligators may live 60 to 80 years.

4. Crocodiles are found in 91 countries—51 percent of all the countries in the world. However they can live only in warm, wet climates. Therefore there are no crocodiles in Canada, northern Europe, or Russia.

5. In the United States, alligators outnumber crocodiles by about 1000 to 1. In fact only about 500 wild crocodiles remain on the whole continent. For that reason crocodiles are considered to be an endangered species and are protected by law.

Copyright © 2003 by Pearson Education, Inc.

Edit the following sentences for the correct use of commas. There are eleven errors. (*For help, see pages 203–204 of the Handbook.*)

EXAMPLE

I bought apples, bananas, carrots, and a melon at the supermarket.

A mother is picking up her daughter from school at the end of the day.

1. "How are you, sweetheart?" the mother asked.

2. "Tired hungry stressed and overworked" the daughter replied. "I can't wait for the weekend."

3. The mother inquired "Do you have much homework tonight?"

4. "Some" said the daughter. "I have to finish a book report, and study for a huge Spanish test."

5. "Mrs. Carlin called and asked, if you can babysit Friday evening" the mother said.

6. "No way" the daughter answered. "This Friday night I'm staying home watching TV, and going to bed early."

7. "You said that you wanted to babysit every week earn money and go shopping at the end of the month" the mother said.

8. "I know" the daughter said "but I can babysit next Friday, and Saturday."

Copyright © 2003 by Pearson Education, Inc.

25g   Other uses of commas

A. Add six commas in the following form. (*For help, see pages 205–207 of the Handbook.*)

CREDIT CARD APPLICATION

Name (last, first):   Tanaka Hiroshi

Date of birth: May 7 1975

Place of birth: Kobe Japan

Address: 3482 Rodeo Drive Beverly Hills California 90210

Occupation: Investment banker

Annual salary: $175000

B. Add five commas in the following note.

Dear Daddy

I went to the mall with Juni and didn't have time to walk the dog. Could you do it please? I promise to do it tomorrow and the next day. Oh I also promise to wash your car like I said I would.

Thanks Dad. I'll be back around 10.

Love & kisses

Lisa

P.S. Juni's cell phone # is 323-947-4738.

   Copyright © 2003 by Pearson Education, Inc.

A. Add semicolons and commas to the following sentences. (*For help, see pages 208–210 of the Handbook.*)

EXAMPLE

The children had left the back door open again; the kitchen was full of flies.

1. My living room is furnished with a carpet that I bought in Turkey a leather sofa and armchair inherited from my grandmother a wonderful floor lamp found at a garage sale and photos of four generations of my family.

2. The room reflects a variety of styles for example the couch is contemporary, but one of the paintings is more than one hundred years old.

3. My piano was imported from Germany my bookcases were handmade by my uncle.

B. Eliminate all the semicolons in the following paragraph by combining sentences, adding transitions, and/or changing the punctuation. (*For help, see pages 208–210 of the Handbook.*)

On Friday night my roommate and I went to a movie; we returned to our apartment around 11:00 p.m. As we approached our front door we could tell something was wrong; the front door was open. Entering cautiously, we immediately saw that the place had been burglarized. In the living room all our books and CDs lay scattered on the floor; the furniture had been overturned; there was glass everywhere; the television was gone. We went next door and called the police immediately; they did not arrive until two hours later.

Copyright © 2003 by Pearson Education, Inc.

Edit the following sentences for the correct use of colons. (*For help, see pages 210–212 of the Handbook.*)

EXAMPLE

There are only three foods I refuse to eat : liver, spinach, and oysters.

1. Please bring the following items to every class a pencil or pen, an eraser, lined paper, your textbook, and a dictionary.

2. Your essay has two qualities that I admire excellent writing and thought-provoking ideas.

3. My father's favorite saying was the following "It is better to keep your mouth shut and be thought a fool than to open it and remove all doubt."

4. When I go to college, I plan to major in: engineering, computer science, or physics.

5. My grandmother, who became a widow at an early age, had two prized possessions her wedding ring and a love letter from her husband.

6. My favorite nineteenth-century American authors are: Mark Twain and Walt Whitman.

7. Last night we rented the movie *Austin Powers The Spy Who Shagged Me.*

8. We always take a break at 2.50 p.m.

9. The colors of the Italian flag are: green, white, and red.

10. This cake has only six ingredients flour, sugar, eggs, oil, baking powder, and salt.

Copyright © 2003 by Pearson Education, Inc.

28a Apostrophes with possessives

Change each item into a possessive phrase containing an apostrophe or an apostrophe + -s. (*For help, see pages 213–215 of the Handbook.*)

EXAMPLE

the boyfriend of Rose ___Rose's boyfriend___

1. the diameter of the earth _____

2. the height of the mountains _____

3. the surface of the table _____

4. the legs of the chairs _____

5. the room of the mother and father _____

6. the play area of the children _____

7. the mother of my sister-in-law _____

8. the schedules of Mrs. Allen and Mrs. Ellis _____

9. the home of the queen of England _____

10. the speeches of the politicians _____

11. the policy of the UN (United Nations) _____

12. the responsibility of nobody _____

Edit the following sentences for the correct use of apostrophes. Some sentences have more than one error. (*For help, see pages 213–217 of the Handbook.*)

EXAMPLE

Today is the president's wife's birthday.

1. Its a beautiful day.

2. The angry mans car was towed because he had parked in a no-parking zone.

3. My daughters two best friend's birthday's are on the same day.

4. Yesterday I bought three CD's and spent the evening listening to music.

5. I received a catalogue advertising mens' shoes.

6. The government reaffirmed it's policy to provide free education for all citizens.

7. Last Friday we were invited to the Thomas's.

8. Tonight we're having dinner at the Baker's.

9. Her handwriting is unclear. I can't tell the difference between her Ms and Ns.

10. Feeling lonely, Agnes ate a whole box of chocolate's by herself.

11. If you don't proofread your essay, its going to be full of spelling mistakes.

12. **A:** Wheres your math book?

    B: I don't know. Can I borrow your's?

Copyright © 2003 by Pearson Education, Inc.

Edit the following sentences for the correct use of quotation marks. Change small letters to capital letters where necessary. The first sentence is punctuated for you as an example. (*For help, see pages 217–219 of the Handbook.*)

1. The other day my eight-year-old son asked me the following question: "Why do dogs in books always say '*bow wow*'?"

2. What do you think their bark sounds like? I asked him.

3. It depends, he said. If the dog is big, I think it sounds like *woof-woof*. But little dogs sound like they're saying *arf-arf*.

4. Did you know, I responded, that people around the world imitate animals sounds in different ways?

5. Huh? he replied.

6. I explained, for example, in Spanish, dogs say *guau guau*. In Hebrew, it's *hav hav*, and in Japanese, it's *wan wan* or *kyan kyan*.

7. But don't animals make the same sounds everywhere? he asked, puzzled.

8. Of course they do, I answered. But speakers of different languages express the sounds differently.

9. That's so funny! my son exclaimed. Where'd you hear about this?

10. On a radio program called Pet Talk; I heard it in the car on my way to work.

Copyright © 2003 by Pearson Education, Inc.

Add parentheses and dashes to the following sentences. In some sentences, replace commas. (*For help, see pages 220–221 of the Handbook.*)

EXAMPLE

Slowly and carefully, the child placed each toy in the box ̄then picked up the

box and dumped it on the floor.

1. The procedure for guessing unfamiliar words is as follows: a read the whole
   sentence in which the word appears; b determine the part of speech of the
   unfamiliar word; c look in the sentence for clues to the meaning; d think of a
   word or phrase that fits in the sentence instead of the unfamiliar word.

2. Abraham Lincoln 1809-1865 was the sixteenth president of the United States.

3. We spent all day Saturday from 8:00 a.m. to 6:00 p.m. working in the garden.

4. Jerusalem is a holy city to three major religions Judaism, Christianity, and
   Islam.

5. The famous actor owned a Porsche, a Mercedes, a Jaguar, a Ferrari and a 1968
   Volkswagen Beetle, a gift from his father when he was eighteen years old.

6. Danny Please remember to put the dog outside before you leave. Make sure
   there's water in his bowl.

7. Some fruits peaches, avocados, plums, apricots will ripen faster if you keep
   them inside a paper bag.

Copyright © 2003 by Pearson Education, Inc.

33 Capital Letters

Edit the following items for capitalization errors. There are sixty-nine errors.
(*For help, see pages 224–229 of the Handbook.*)

1. karen andres is the Student Advisor at the english language institute.

2. dear ms. andres:

   last friday I dropped off my Résumé, but unfortunately it contained an error.

   here is a corrected copy. could you please remove the old one from my file and

   replace it with this one? thank you.

   yours truly,

   Lorena Cardozo

3. *See Lorena Cardozo's résumé on page 118.*

Copyright © 2003 by Pearson Education, Inc.

Résumé

Lorena Cardozo

401 second avenue

hollywood, california 90049

Desired Position: Teaching intern, oak elementary school

Education: university of california, riverside: ma, Education,[1]
2004 (expected)

california state university, northridge: ba, spanish, 2002

Teaching Experience: Teaching assistant, psychology 101, fall semester 2003

spanish language tutor, 1998 to present

Other Experience: Intern at *los angeles times* newspaper, summer 2001

Volunteer at Daycare Center, kraft corp., 1999

Camp counselor, roxbury park, summer 1996–1998

Additional Skills: Languages: spanish, french (fluent), arabic (beginner)

Music: I play the Guitar and sing

Travel: north america, western europe, and the middle east

Interests: renaissance art and music; folk dancing; ethnic cooking

References: Available from

university career center

california state university, northridge

18233 norton avenue

northridge, ca 91330

---

[1]It is acceptable in a résumé to capitalize names of university majors.

Copyright © 2003 by Pearson Education, Inc.

Edit the following sentences for hyphen errors. Some items have more than one error. (*For help, see pages 230–232 of the Handbook.*)

EXAMPLE

left-handed
My daughter is the only ~~left-handed~~ person in our family.

1. My sister in law is studying for a Ph.D. in literature. Her dissertation deals

   with postmodern poetry.

2. Being criticized in front of others can be damaging to a child's self esteem.

3. My brother and his exwife still talk to each other almost every day.

4. Thanks to his excellent grades and test scores, Yoshi got into Harvard

   University.

5. Doctors and dentists advise pregnant women not to have Xrays taken.

6. My cousin was six-feet-tall by the time he was fourteen.

7. They bought a two door car with four wheel drive.

8. The cake recipe calls for three fourths of a cup of butter.

9. Aren't you ashamed to turn in such a badly-written essay?

10. The teacher gave the students a five minute warning before instructing them

    to put down their pencils and hand in their exam papers.

11. One of the things I admire about movie director Steven Spielberg is his imagi-

    nation.

12. They have a good tempered, sweet dog and an unfriendly, mean cat.

Copyright © 2003 by Pearson Education, Inc.

Underline words where necessary in the following sentences. Three sentences are correct. (*For help, see pages 233–235 of the Handbook.*)

EXAMPLE

The most popular newspaper in the United States is <u>USA Today</u>.

1. One of the largest passenger ships ever built, the Queen Mary was purchased in 1967 by the city of Long Beach, California, where it is a popular tourist attraction.

2. The most profitable movie ever made was Titanic, which won eleven Academy Awards in 1998.

3. As part of the wedding reception, the groom took the microphone and sang "You Are the Sunshine of My Life" to his new bride.

4. Mrs. Park keeps track of her students' test scores using an Excel spreadsheet.

5. The first time I saw the Mona Lisa, by Leonardo da Vinci, I was surprised that the famous painting was so small.

6. Every Christmas, the ballet The Nutcracker, by Peter Illich Tchaikovsky, is broadcast on American television.

7. My daughter is a picky eater. The only things she likes to eat for dinner are spaghetti, burritos, and chicken.

8. The current issue of National Geographic online has an article called "Inside the Tornado" about a man who chases tornadoes to collect scientific data.

9. Americans are fond of self-help books. One of the earliest and most famous books was How to Win Friends and Influence People, by Dale Carnegie.

10. The names of four generations of children are written in our family Bible.

  Copyright © 2003 by Pearson Education, Inc.

Edit the following sentences to correct errors in abbreviations. Some items have more than one error, and two sentences have no errors. (*For help, see pages 236–240 of the Handbook.*)

EXAMPLE

November   *United States*
~~Nov.~~ 11, Veteran's Day, is a national holiday in the ~~U.S.~~

1. In the fall she will be attending Johns Hopkins Univ. in Baltimore, MD, where she plans to major in French lit.

2. Electric cars such as the EV1 can easily travel up to eighty mph.

3. It will cost ca. $2 million to build a new wing on the Y.M.C.A. building.

4. Ms Estee Lauder, who was born in 1908, founded the famous cosmetics corp. of the same name during the Depression.

5. I hate getting up early, so this semester I have all my classes in the PM.

6. The sun is about 150 million km from the earth.

7. Several senators had to wait two days for an appt. with the pres.

8. Dr Condoleeza Rice, PhD, is National Security Affairs advisor to President George W. Bush.

9. During World War II, the Allied forces fighting against Germany consisted of the U.S., the U.K., and France.

10. My name is Soo-Jung Park, and I come from KOREA. This year I am studying English in LA, CA, in the USA.

11. By the year 2002, almost 25 million people had died of AIDS since it first appeared in the 1980s.

12. In our house we have a TV, a VCR, a CD player, a DVD player, and three computers. My daughter rarely uses any of them; she would rather read a book.

Copyright © 2003 by Pearson Education, Inc.

Edit the following sentences to correct errors in writing numbers. (*For help, see pages 240–243 of the Handbook.*)

EXAMPLE

There are 3ʘ28 feet in a meter.

1. The most successful pop singing group in history is The Beatles. They have sold more than 1,000,000,000[1] records worldwide.

2. Tom Leppard, a retired soldier who lives in Scotland, has tattoos on ninety-nine % of his body.

3. 3 dogs have given birth to 23 puppies each.

4. The country with the largest population is China, with almost 1.3 billions people.

5. The world's deepest lake is Lake Baikal in Russia. It contains 1/5 of the world's fresh water.

6. The average Japanese man lives more than 77 years, while the average woman lives nearly eighty-four years.

7. The world's largest religious group is the Roman Catholic Church, which has 17,4% of the world's population.

8. All fourteen of the world's eight-thousand-meter mountain peaks are in the Himalaya range.

9. The world's largest train station is Grand Central Terminal in New York City, built between nineteen-o-three and nineteen-thirteen.

10. The first photographic image of the dark side of the moon was recorded at six-thirty a.m. on October 7, 1959, from a distance of 7 thousand kilometers, by the Soviet spacecraft *Luna III.*

---

[1]All statistics are from *The Guinness Book of World Records,* http://www.guinnessrecords.com

 Copyright © 2003 by Pearson Education, Inc.

A. Correct one misspelled word in each group. (*For help, see pages 244–250 of the Handbook.*)

EXAMPLE
foreign
~~foriegn~~, receipt, relieve, weight

1. smiling, sensible, comparison, lateest

2. rudely, useful, hopless, politeness

3. nineth, truly, placement, awful

4. lately, grayish, tryed, happily

5. hurrying, playing, arriveing, confusing

6. dropped, sitting, writen, boxes

7. prefered, regretted, permitting, beginning

B. Write the plural form of the following nouns. Remember: A few nouns have no plural form. (*For help, see pages 244–250 of the Handbook.*)

1. table _____

2. watch _____

3. dictionary _____

4. toy _____

5. shelf _____

6. tomato _____

7. zero _____

8. woman _____

9. person _____

10. sheep _____

11. pants _____

12. medium _____

13. father-in-law _____

14. 1000 _____

15. BA _____

16. M.D. _____

(*continued on next page*)

Copyright © 2003 by Pearson Education, Inc.

17. d (the letter) _____

18. statistics _____

19. alto _____

20. potato _____

21. stress _____

22. news _____

23. calf _____

24. child _____

Copyright © 2003 by Pearson Education, Inc.

Complete the following outline by filling in the blank lines with an appropriate word or group of words. There are many possible ways to complete the outline. (*For help, see pages 261–263 of the Handbook.*)

I. Introduction

Thesis: There are both advantages and disadvantages to living in a large city such as Tokyo or New York.

II. _____

   A. Cultural opportunities

      1. theaters

      2. museums

      3. _____

      4. _____

   B. Educational opportunities

      1. large number of colleges and universities

      2. _____

   C. _____

      1. most large companies have their headquarters in large cities

      2. many businesses provide services to city residents

(*continued on next page*)

Copyright © 2003 by Pearson Education, Inc.

III. _____

   A. _____

      1. traffic jams

      2. crowded buses

      3. _____

   B. Expensive

      1. _____

      2. _____

   C. Impersonal

      1. people don't know their neighbors

      2. _____

IV. Conclusion

Copyright © 2003 by Pearson Education, Inc.

A. Use the following guidelines to revise the paragraph. (*For help, see pages 255–270 of the Handbook.*)

1. Rewrite the title. It should not be a complete sentence.
2. Expand and rewrite the topic sentence.
3. Decide whether any main points need to be expanded or shortened.
4. Delete two sentences that do not support the main idea.
5. Check all transitions. Consider expanding some of them.
6. Rewrite the conclusion so that it restates the main idea of the paragraph.

San Francisco Is a Nice City

San Francisco is a nice city. First, it has many famous tourist attractions such as the cable cars, Chinatown, Alcatraz Island, and Union Square. Second, it has world-famous restaurants which feature every imaginable type of ethnic food as well as outstanding fish dishes. Most meals in San Francisco are served with a unique type of bread called "sourdough." Though many people think it tastes strange at first, they soon develop a taste for it. That's why many tourists leaving from San Francisco International Airport can be seen boarding their planes with a loaf of bread under their arm. One more thing worth noting about San Francisco's restaurants is that they are known for their excellent service. The servers are courteous and professional, and patrons are treated like honored guests. However, I ate at one restaurant in Chinatown where the service was terrible. The third thing that makes San Francisco a great vacation city is its geographical situation. The city is small—only forty-nine square miles. The ocean surrounds it on three sides, and there are many hills. Consequently, beautiful views of the water and the downtown skyscrapers can be seen from many places in the city. In conclusion, you should visit San Francisco.

B. Find and correct ten errors in this paragraph from a student essay. (*For help, see pages 255–270 of the Handbook.*)

Traffic Problems in Seoul, Korea

Seoul, Korea, have one of highest traffic accident rates in the world, however, it's penalties for traffic violations and its automobile insurance rates are among the lowest. I believe that if the government increased the fines for traffic violation, fewer people would causing traffic problems. Furthermore, an increase in automobile insurance rates would make people think twice about owning a car. An other traffic regulation that could reduce the number of automobiles is one the government used during the Olympic Games in Seoul. It is a regulation whereby only certain automobiles can be on the road on a certain day according to their license plate numbers. For example, on Monday Wednesday and Friday only those automobiles with license plate numbers ending with an odd number can be on the road. And on Tuesday, Thursday, and Saturday, only cars with even-numbered plates.

Copyright © 2003 by Pearson Education, Inc.

Read the following paragraph. Then choose the best topic sentence for it from the choices listed. (*For help, see page 273 of the Handbook.*)

_____. The most important change has been the increase in the divorce rate. Now, approximately 50% of all marriages end in divorce. Naturally, this has had some important consequences. First, the number of single-parent families—both single mothers and single fathers—has risen dramatically. Many women who never worked before or did not work while they were married have had to go to work. Single fathers, on the other hand, have had a different problem to deal with. In the past, it was customary for children of divorced parents to live with their mother. But now, many divorced fathers have started to insist on their right to share in the raising of their children. The result in many cases is an arrangement called "joint custody," which gives both parents the legal right to have their children live with them part of the time.

Possible topic sentences

1. The American family faces many challenges in the twenty-first century.
2. The weakening of traditional values and the empowerment of women have both contributed to a dramatic increase in the U.S. divorce rate.
3. The United States has one of the highest divorce rates in the world.
4. The American family has undergone significant transformations in the last thirty years.

Copyright © 2003 by Pearson Education, Inc.

Read the topic sentence. Then place a check mark next to six sentences that provide good support. Put an X next to sentences that provide poor support because they are not facts, because they are not appropriate, or because they are not relevant. (*For help, see pages 274–276 of the Handbook.*)

Topic sentence: Cellist Yo Yo Ma is not only one of the most brilliant but also one of the most beloved musicians in the world today.

Possible supporting sentences

_____ 1. The cello is a very difficult instrument to master.

_____ 2. He has performed as soloist with symphony orchestras around the world, including those of Boston, Toronto, New York, Israel, and the Los Angeles Philharmonic.

_____ 3. Born October 7, 1955, to Chinese parents living in Paris, he began playing the cello at the age of four.

_____ 4. Yo Yo Ma is a genius.

_____ 5. The *Los Angeles Times* described Ma as "an artist possessing tremendous technical brilliance and musicality."[1]

_____ 6. Ma has made many recordings and won many awards.

_____ 7. Ma has recorded over 45 albums and won 14 Grammy Awards.[2]

_____ 8. Ma is known for his ability to play in a variety of musical styles.

_____ 9. Yo Yo Ma is an amazingly diverse artist, famous not only for his performances of classical music but also for his participation in projects involving other musical styles such as jazz, country, and traditional Chinese folk music.

_____ 10. Yo Yo Ma is married and has two children.

_____ 11. Once Ma accidentally left his cello in the trunk of a taxi he was riding in.

_____ 12. Yo Yo Ma has played the cello in such hit films as *Crouching Tiger, Hidden Dragon* and *Seven Years in Tibet.*

---

[1]*Los Angeles Times,* February 1996.
[2]Grammy Awards are given annually to outstanding musicians in a variety of categories.

Copyright © 2003 by Pearson Education, Inc.

Edit the following paragraphs for unity. Cross out two sentences that are off the topic. (*For help, see page 277 of the Handbook.*)

The History of Corn

Corn is a plant that is native to the Western Hemisphere. The Indians of North and South America had been growing corn for thousands of years before Columbus arrived in the New World in 1492. Indeed, fossils of ancient corn cobs can be found in museums today. When Columbus's ships landed in the West Indies, he traded with the natives there and took corn back with him to Spain. From there, corn was introduced to other western European countries and eventually to the rest of the world.

When the first European settlers came to the New World, the Indians gave them corn to eat, thereby saving them from near-certain starvation during their first harsh winter in America. The Indians called this life-saving food "ma-hiz," which the settlers pronounced as "maize." Later, the Indians taught the settlers how to plant corn and use it in the preparation of various foods. Corn was so valuable in those days that it was used as a form of money and traded for meat and furs. Today the United States grows about 80% of the world's corn and is the world's largest exporter.[1]

---

[1] *Source:* "The Many Uses of Corn," Ohio Corn Marketing Program, http://www.ohiocorn.org/about_use_many.htm

Copyright © 2003 by Pearson Education, Inc.

Improve the coherence of this paragraph by adding appropriate transition signals. Choose from the transition signals in parentheses. Sometimes the punctuation before or after a blank will help you choose. Circle your choice. (*For help, see pages 278–282 of the Handbook.*)

Are you a shy person? If so, you are not alone. According to research by Dr. Philip Zimbardo of Stanford University, more than 40% of Americans say they are shy in most situations, (**1**) _____ (*in addition / and / however*) another 15% say they are shy in certain situations. (**2**) _____ (*Although / In contrast / While*), only 5% say they have never experienced shyness.

Dr. Zimbardo distinguishes between two kinds of shyness. (**3**) _____ (*First / The first / A more important*) kind is called "situational" shyness. As the name suggests, this is the temporary kind of shyness that most people feel if, (**4**) _____ (*for example / such as / like*), they meet an attractive person for the first time or if they have to speak in public. (**5**) _____ (*In contrast / As a result / In other words*), this kind of shyness is caused by external circumstances. (**6**) _____ (*By the way / Next / On the other hand*), some people are born shy and feel shy all the time, in nearly every situation. For such people, shyness can lead to a variety of negative consequences. (**7**) _____ (*For instance / In brief / Consequently*), shy people have fewer friends and are more likely to be depressed than outgoing people.

If shyness is a problem for you, what can you do about it? Dr. Zimbardo has a number of recommendations. (**8**) _____ (*Also / Moreover / First*), it may help to remember that nearly half of all people are shy like you. If you are in a social situation (**9**) _____ (*for example / like / meanwhile*) a party, try to find other shy people and talk to them. Start the conversation by admitting that you are shy.

Copyright © 2003 by Pearson Education, Inc.

(**10**) _____ (*As a result / Nevertheless / Otherwise*), they may assume you are boring or not interested in them.

(**11**) _____ (*Because / Because of / Therefore*) shyness can be a crippling problem for so many people, Dr. Zimbardo and his colleagues at Stanford started the Shyness Institute, devoted to research into the causes and treatment of this important condition.

Copyright © 2003 by Pearson Education, Inc.

Read the following paragraph. Then choose the best concluding sentence from the choices listed. (*For help, see page 283 of the Handbook.*)

Cockroaches have lived on the earth for more than 400 million years. What accounts for the amazing survival of this hated insect? First of all, cockroaches are very adaptable and can be found almost everywhere: outdoors in tropical climates and indoors in cooler ones. With their preference for warm, humid places, cockroaches naturally seek out areas in homes and factories where food is prepared and stored. Another characteristic favoring the survival of the cockroach is that it eats almost anything. Originally cockroaches were scavengers of decaying plant materials, but their diet now includes items as diverse as "human" food, dead insects, paper, and even glue. Finally, cockroaches, though small, have few natural enemies. Not only do they give off a bad smell, but eating them causes birds and

animals to get sick. _____.

Possible concluding sentences

1. These three reasons explain why humans hate cockroaches so much that they spend millions of dollars each year to exterminate them.
2. These three reasons explain why cockroaches will probably exist on this planet long after our own species disappears.
3. These three reasons explain why cockroaches are commonly found in kitchens all over the world.

Copyright © 2003 by Pearson Education, Inc.

A. The sentences in the following introductory paragraph are in scrambled order. Number the sentences in the correct order. Place the thesis statement last. Sentence 1 is numbered for you. (*For help, see pages 291–294 of the Handbook.*)

_____ **a.** If you live in an urban area almost anywhere in the world, chances are that you have not.

_____ **b.** Today, in most of the world's cities and even in many suburban and rural areas, fewer than one hundred stars are visible in the night sky.

__1__ **c.** Have you ever seen a night sky filled from horizon to horizon with thousands of brightly shining stars?

_____ **d.** In addition to obstructing our view of the stars, light pollution creates dangerous driving conditions, robs people of their privacy, and has negative effects on our health.

_____ **e.** The reason for this reduced visibility is the phenomenon known as light pollution.

_____ **f.** Light pollution occurs when too much artificial light enters the night sky and reflects off water droplets and dust particles in the air, resulting in a night sky that is never truly dark.

B. Follow the same instructions as in Part A.

_____ **a.** Examples include ads for low-rate mortgages, credit cards, investment tips, herbal remedies, and pornography.

_____ **b.** According to ABC News,[1] the average Internet user receives more than 600 spam messages a year, and this number may jump to nearly 1,500 by the year 2006.

_____ **c.** *Spam* is the English word for those unwanted advertisements that arrive in your e-mailbox almost every day.

_____ **d.** However, thanks to programs developed by a number of companies, there are already some steps you can take to reduce this form of electronic trash.

---

[1]http://abcnews.go.com/sections/scitech/DailyNews/spamfilters020619.html

Copyright © 2003 by Pearson Education, Inc. **135**

Read the following introduction. Then choose the best conclusion from the choices listed. (*For help, see pages 296–297 of the Handbook.*)

In the United States, students at private independent and religious schools have always worn uniforms, while students in public schools have not been required to do so. This trend is changing, however. More and more public schools across the nation, including the influential New York City school system with its 550,000 elementary school children, are requiring students to wear uniforms for a number of reasons. Most important, they say, is that uniforms eliminate competition based on clothing, leaving students freer to focus on their studies instead of their appearance. In addition, statistics prove that schools that require uniforms have fewer robberies and assaults over expensive clothes, shoes, and jewelry. A third advantage of uniforms is that they are cheaper and more convenient for parents and students alike.

Possible conclusions

1. In conclusion, uniforms offer advantages to schools, to parents, and to students. There are additional advantages as well. One study showed that students who wear uniforms get higher grades and better evaluations from their teachers than students who choose their own wardrobe. Thus, uniforms are associated with greater success in school and in life. All these factors explain why a majority of people surveyed favor requiring uniforms in their children's schools.

2. In conclusion, uniforms offer advantages to schools, to parents, and to students. Schools benefit from improved safety and an atmosphere that promotes learning instead of competition based on clothing. Parents benefit from the reduced cost of uniforms, and students benefit from their convenience. All these factors explain why a majority of people surveyed favor requiring uniforms in their children's schools.

3. In conclusion, uniforms offer clear advantages to schools, to parents, and to students. Nevertheless, there are also disadvantages to requiring them. The United States is a country that has always valued individual expression and freedom of choice. These values are stifled when students wear uniforms. For this reason, I do not feel that uniforms should be required in public schools, despite the advantages. I think a better policy would be to make them optional rather than mandatory.

Copyright © 2003 by Pearson Education, Inc.

ANSWER KEY

PART I   The Basics

1a   Nouns, pages 1–2

PRACTICE 1
1. Circle: Olympics, Salt Lake City, Utah
2. Underline: ceremonies
   Circle: February
3. Underline: flame, plane
   Circle: United States, Athens, Greece
4. Underline: flame, country, foot, plane, train, ship, dogsled, snowmobile
5. Underline: events, skating, skating, snowboarding, skiing
6. Underline: event, skeleton, kind, bobsledding
   Circle: Olympics
7. Underline: number, medals
   Circle: Germany

PRACTICE 2
1. Underline: plants, animals
   Circle: oxygen, life
2. Underline: people
   Circle: love
3. Underline: students
   Circle: homework
4. Underline: shirts, hat
   Circle: paint
5. Underline: suitcases
   Circle: luggage
6. Underline: song
   Circle: music
7. Underline: roses, garden, week
   Circle: water
8. Underline: poodle, dog
   Circle: hair

1b   Pronouns, pages 3–4

1. **A:** Could <u>you</u> pick up <u>my</u> gray suit from the dry cleaner today? <u>I</u> need to wear <u>it</u> tomorrow.
   B: <u>I</u>'m really sorry, but <u>this</u> is a busy day for <u>me</u>. <u>I</u>'m afraid <u>you</u> 'll have to pick <u>it</u> up <u>yourself</u>.
   A: <u>That</u>'s impossible. <u>I</u>'m going to be in meetings from 8:00 a.m. until 6:00 p.m.
   B: Can <u>you</u> wear <u>your</u> dark blue suit instead of the gray <u>one</u>?
   A: <u>Which</u> dark blue suit?
   B: <u>You</u> know, the <u>one</u> that <u>you</u> got for <u>your</u> brother's wedding.

A: Oh, *that* suit. <u>I</u> forgot all about <u>it</u>. <u>It</u>'s kind of formal, don't <u>you</u> think?
B: Maybe a little. But <u>it</u> looks wonderful on <u>you</u>.

2. People say that dogs and cats are natural enemies, but <u>my</u> dog, Ralph, and <u>my</u> cat, Rex, are very good friends. <u>I</u> got <u>them</u> two years ago from a friend <u>who</u> had to move to a different city. At first <u>they</u> were shy with <u>me</u>, but after a few days (and a few meals!), <u>we</u> all started to feel comfortable together.
   Ralph and Rex are both entertaining and interesting to watch. For example, <u>they</u> love to lick <u>one another</u>, and it's quite funny to watch <u>them</u> taking a "bath" <u>this</u> way. <u>My</u> pets also seem to enjoy looking at <u>themselves</u> in the mirror. <u>I</u> wonder: Do <u>they</u> recognize <u>themselves</u>, or do <u>they</u> think <u>they</u> 're seeing a different cat and dog? <u>Another</u> one of <u>their</u> favorite activities is looking out the front window. <u>They</u> get very excited whenever <u>anybody</u> walks by, especially if <u>it</u>'s <u>another</u> dog or cat.
   <u>I</u> don't know if animals have feelings like people do, but if <u>they</u> do, then it's clear that Ralph and Rex love <u>each other</u>. To tell <u>you</u> the truth, <u>they</u> get along better than a lot of people <u>I</u> know!

1c   Verbs, page 5

1. **A:** You <u>seem</u> ^{MV} quiet this morning.
   B: Yeah, well, I'<u>m</u> ^{MV} worried about my mother.
   A: What <u>happened</u> ^{MV} to her?
   B: She <u>broke</u> ^{MV} her leg, and she'<u>s</u> ^{HV} <u>having</u> ^{MV} a hard time getting around. I <u>want</u> ^{MV} to help her, but she <u>says</u> ^{MV} she'<u>s</u> fine and she doesn't ^{HV} <u>want</u> ^{MV} any help.
   A: She <u>sounds</u> ^{MV} like a very independent person.
   B: Yes, she <u>is</u> ^{MV}. But ever since my father <u>died</u> ^{MV}, I <u>know</u> ^{MV} she'<u>s</u> ^{HV} <u>been</u> ^{MV} pretty lonely.

Copyright © 2003 by Pearson Education, Inc.

137

2. **A:** *HV* Do you *MV* like sports?

   B: It *MV* depends. I *MV* like playing a few sports, and I *MV* like watching others.

   A: What *HV* do you *MV* like to play?

   B: Mainly volleyball and soccer. Oh, and swimming. I *MV* love to swim.

   A: Me too! In fact, I *HV* was *MV* planning to go to the pool tonight. *HV* Do you *MV* want to come too?

   B: What time *HV* are you *MV* planning to go? I *HV* have to *MV* finish a report for my literature class before I *HV* can *MV* do anything else.

   A: I *HV* was *MV* thinking about 8:00 p.m.

   B: *HV* Can you *MV* make it a little later, like 9:00?

   A: Sure. I'*HV*ll *MV* come by at 9:00, and we'*HV*ll *MV* walk over to the gym together.

Id Adjectives, page 6

Adjective	Noun modified
1. professional	writer
quiet	world
my, clear	mind
2. ready	I
Several	times
small	notebook
some	pencils
coffee	shop
my	home
3. pleasant	experience
ten-minute	walk
fresh	air
my, friendly	neighbors
colorful	gardens
4. heavenly	smell
roasted	coffee
my	nose
5. furnished	Josie's
soft,	sofas
comfortable	
6. my	work
interesting,	people
unusual	
fascinating	conversations

Ie Articles, page 7

1. a, the, a	5. a, an, a, a	8. The, a
2. a	6. A, an,	9. an, a, a
3. the, a	the	10. an
4. the, the, a	7. a	

If Adverbs, page 8

Adverb	Word modified
1. very	early
2. here	put
over	there
there	put
3. very	sorry
again	forgotten
4. almost	always
always	eats
5. perfectly	speaks
fairly	well
well	speaks
badly	speaks
6. loudly	talking
clearly	hear
7. cautiously	approached
8. outside	stood
patiently	waiting
9. daily	change
10. very	tired
lately	feeling
really	need

Ig Prepositions, page 9

1. at, of
2. inside, to, because of
3. in, up, in, on, on, except for, of, for
4. unlike, In, on, under, to, with, on
5. in, with, of, of, of, for
6. up with, to
7. to, out, or
8. With, for, above
9. with, with

Ih Conjunctions, page 10

1. and
2. not only, but also
3. and, and
4. Unless, however
5. if, and, Then
6. whereas
7. so that
8. but
9. Besides, both, and
10. Consequently, and
11. and, and, also

Copyright © 2003 by Pearson Education, Inc.

3b Dependent clauses, pages 11–12

1. how we are going to divide up the work
2. that need to be done
3. who will bring Jack to the party
4. While we're eating, After Jack and I finish eating, that I need to stop by your apartment, because I left my guitar there, as soon as we arrive
5. what we're going to eat and drink
6. if you tell me, where to buy it
7. where the Cake Factory is, where Sofie's mother works, so that you can find a parking place
8. no dependent clause
9. If people want beer or wine
10. that we also have snacks like chips and nuts and maybe some fruit
11. When I call the guests

4a Sentence parts, page 13

1. ss thousands of these animals
2. only an estimated 300 to 500 of them
3. The remaining seals
4. hunting for the seals' skins
5. the greatest threats
6. A variety of national laws and species-protection programs
7. Protected areas
8. the number of people
9. a unique natural treasure

PART 2 Clear Sentences

6a Making compound sentences, pages 14–15

1. Many people believe the myth that bats suck people's blood; *as a result,* they are terrified of bats.
2. In fact, most species of bats do not eat blood, *nor do they* carry the disease rabies, another common myth.
3. Seventy percent of the world's bat species eat only insects, *so* they are extremely helpful animals.

4. In the winter, bats in cold climates migrate to warmer places, *or* they hibernate in caves.
5. A small percentage of bats feed on the blood of warm-blooded animals such as birds, horses, and cattle; *they* are called "vampire" bats.
6. Vampire bats are extremely rare, *yet* they are the most famous type of bat.
7. Another myth about bats is that they sometimes fly into people's hair; *however,* this is also completely untrue.
8. Bats, like humans, are warm-blooded mammals. *Moreover,* they have hair and give birth to living young.
9. Most bats are very small, weighing less than 100 grams; *nevertheless,* they can live as long as thirty years.
10. Bats, which are fascinating animals, are not dangerous, *nor are they* aggressive.

6b Connecting words with coordinating conjunctions, page 16

1. but/yet	5. and	9. but/yet
2. or	6. and	10. or
3. and	7. and	11. or
4. and	8. or	

6c Connecting words with correlative conjunctions, pages 17–18

1. not only	7. either	11. either
2. but also	8. or	12. or
3. either	9. not only/	13. neither
4. or	both	14. nor
5. Both	10. but also/	
6. and	and	

6d Using parallel forms, page 19

It is my pleasure to write this letter of recommendation for Ms. Maria Castro, who was a student in my American Short Stories for International Students course during the spring semester of 2003. The course required students to read famous American short stories and *to interact* with the texts. In all areas—reading, speaking, and *writing*—Maria was one of the best students I have ever had. Her comments, not only *spoken* but also written, were original, intelligent, *and often* funny. Whenever I asked a question in class,

Copyright © 2003 by Pearson Education, Inc.

Maria usually had an answer, yet *she* listened carefully to other students' ideas too. Therefore, Maria was well-liked and *admired* by her classmates. Because of her intelligence, her strong motivation to learn, and *her* excellent language skills, I am confident Maria can succeed as a full-time student at your university.

If you have additional questions about this student, I would be happy to answer them. Please feel free to contact me either by phone or *by e-mail.*

7a Making complex sentences, pages 20–23

PRACTICE 1
A. 1. Although
   2. after / when
   3. as soon as
   4. so that
   5. when / after
   6. if

B. 1. Don't leave the door open *if* the air conditioner is turned on.
   2. Because I misplaced my car keys, *I* wasn't able to go out today.
   3. Please wash the dishes *before* you put them away in the cupboard.
   4. While the professor spoke, *the* students took notes.
   5. *My* mother said, "*As soon as / After* you finish your homework, you can watch half an hour of television."
   6. We don't need to go to school today *because* it's Saturday.

PRACTICE 2
Note the adjective clauses are underlined, the antecedents are in *italics*, and the relative pronouns and adverbs are in **boldface**.

Vatican City, **which** <u>has an area of only 0.2 square mile</u>, is generally considered to be the world's smallest country. Yet some people say there is a *country* **that** <u>is even smaller than the Vatican</u>. You have probably never heard of it. It is called the Sovereign Military Order of Malta (SMOM). Although it was once an independent country, today it is principally a religious *organization* **that** <u>provides humanitarian and medical assistance all over the world</u>.
   The Order of Malta was founded in *1099*, **when** <u>it established a hospital in Jerusalem to</u> <u>care for sick travelers during the First Crusade</u>. The organization later expanded and built additional hospitals along the route from Europe to the Holy Land. In 1530 it was given the island of *Malta*, <u>from **which** it got its name</u>. In 1834 the organization moved to *Rome*, **where** <u>it still has its headquarters today</u>.
   The Order of Malta currently has about 5,000 members. It is governed by a "Grand Master" and a "*Sovereign Council*," **which** <u>has both permanent and elected *members* **who** accept the authority of the Pope and the Roman Catholic Church</u>.
   Although the order has no territory other than its headquarters in Rome and a fortress in Malta, it is officially recognized by 67 countries. It makes *coins*, **which** <u>do not circulate</u>, and it prints *stamps* **that** <u>are accepted by 45 national post offices</u>. It has been a permanent observer at the United Nations since 1994. Thus, it is unclear whether the Order of Malta can be called the world's smallest nation or not.

PRACTICE 3
A. Ms. Angela White is one of the most respected teachers in our school for several reasons. First, she takes the time to find out <u>who her students are</u> and <u>what they are interested in</u>, and she tries to connect her lessons to her students' lives and interests. Second, her students say <u>that she is very fair</u>. She makes sure <u>that every person in her class gets an equal chance to participate</u>, and she never plays favorites. Next, Ms. White always gives clear instructions so that students understand exactly <u>what they are supposed to do</u>. In addition, she is sensitive to her students' feelings. If they make mistakes, she knows <u>how to correct them</u> so that students do not feel ashamed. One last thing that makes Ms. White such a good teacher is her nice voice. Her students always mention <u>how much they enjoy listening to her</u>.

B. 1. Do you know what *the homework is* for Monday?
   2. **A:** Excuse me, I'm trying to find the post office. Can you tell me how to get there?
      B: Sure. It's at the corner of Olympic Boulevard and First Street. Do you know where *that is*?
      A: Yes, I do. Thanks for your help.

Copyright © 2003 by Pearson Education, Inc.

3. I don't know who directed the movie *Titanic.* / *Who directed the movie Titanic?*

4. If we want to get good seats for the concert, it's essential that we *be* at the auditorium no later than 7:00 p.m.

5. Excuse me, can you tell me what time *it is?*

7b   Using appositives, pages 24–25

A. The appositives and appositive phrases are underlined, and the nouns or noun phrases they rename are in *italics*.

The composer <u>Wolfgang Amadeus Mozart</u> is regarded as one of the greatest musical geniuses who ever lived. He was born in 1756 in the Austrian town of *Salzburg,* <u>a stunningly beautiful city with a long musical history</u>. Mozart's musical gifts became obvious almost immediately. By the age of four, he could already play the piano. He published *his first compositions,* <u>four pieces for violin and harpsichord</u>, before his eighth birthday.

Mozart's father, <u>Leopold</u>, had been a music teacher. However, he quit teaching in order to manage young Wolfgang's career. When Mozart was six, he began playing concerts with *his sister,* <u>Nanerl</u>, who was also a gifted musician. At the age of seven, Mozart was invited to *Vienna,* <u>the capital of Austria</u>, to play for the royal family. From there, his reputation as a genius spread all over Europe.

B. 1. In 1984, a mostly fictional account of Mozart's life was told in the film *Amadeus.* / in a film, *Amadeus.*

2. Much of the film focused on Mozart's rivalry with another composer, Salieri. / with the composer Salieri.

3. no appositive

4. In fact, the cause of Mozart's death at age 35 is not certain. It may have been a fever or a medical condition, uremia, a result of advanced kidney disease.

5. Mozart died before completing his last masterpiece, his unforgettable *Requiem*.

7d   Using shortened adverb clauses, page 26

1. I had never experienced an earthquake before *visiting* California.

2. *Frightened* of water, Mrs. Alvarez never went swimming with her children.

3. While *working* at home one day, I received a phone call from a man *telling* me I had won $10,000 in a contest.

4. Towns *located* near rivers must be prepared for floods in the springtime.

5. When *eating* fish, you should be careful not to swallow any small bones.

6. A person *wishing* to practice law in the United States must first pass a difficult examination *known* as the bar exam.

7. The blond woman, *not realizing* someone else was in the room, picked up a silver letter opener and put it in her purse.

8. I enjoyed watching the children *playing* baseball in the park.

9. Even after *living* / *having lived* in the U.S. for 25 years, my father still had a heavy accent when *speaking* English.

10. The man *arrested* by the police was wanted for robbing banks in three cities.

8a   Fragments, page 27

A. . . . Chinese culture dominates the area. *There are* Chinese restaurants, clothing stores, bakeries, banks, bookstores, gift shops, jewelers, markets, beauty salons, and more. Some of Chinatown's residents have lived there for forty or fifty years, and they have never learned much English *because* they haven't needed it. *It is* possible to get almost any Chinese product or service in Chinatown *without* traveling to China.

B. Los Angeles is an enjoyable city to visit *if* you have a car. If not, you will need to depend on public transportation, *which* is neither fast nor convenient. Los Angeles has a new subway, but it does not travel to most of the popular tourist attractions. There is no system of elevated trains or streetcars. *There are* only buses, and they can take a long time to go anywhere *because* traffic is very heavy, *especially* in the early morning and late afternoon, when people are traveling to and from work.

8b   Run-together sentences, page 28

1. Broccoli is an ancient vegetable. It has been around for more than 2,000 years. (OR Broccoli is an ancient vegetable that has been around for more than 2,000 years.)

Copyright © 2003 by Pearson Education, Inc.

2. The word *broccoli* comes from the Italian word *brocco*, which means an arm or a branch.
3. It is one of the healthiest vegetables. It is rich in vitamins and low in calories. / It is one of the healthiest vegetables because it is rich in vitamins and low in calories.
4. (*Correct*)
5. Broccoli contains a special chemical substance called sulforaphane, which helps reduce the risk of cancer.
6. Broccoli normally grows best in cool climates. Recently new varieties that grow well in mild and subtropical climates have been developed in Taiwan. / Broccoli normally grows best in cool climates, but recently new varieties that grow well in mild or subtropical climates have been developed in Taiwan.
7. Most broccoli varieties are green; however, there are a few that are purple in color.
8. Broccoli is one of the most popular vegetables in the United States; not everyone likes it, however.
9. One famous broccoli hater is George Bush, who was president of the United States from 1989 to 1993.
10. (*Correct*)

8c   Choppy writing, pages 29–30

My first suggestion is that you should build a dormitory next to the school building. We are overseas students, *and* we live far from the school. (OR We are overseas students *who live far from the school.*) Most of us do not have cars, *so* it would be better for us to have rooms close to the school. (OR *Since most of us do not have cars, it* would be better for us to have rooms close to the school.) That would reduce the problems of absence and tardiness.

In addition, you should open a cafeteria in the building. It should have a variety of food and music. It would be *both* convenient *and* relaxing *if* students and teachers could eat together. They could get to know one another better.

You should also add a library *that* can help us in our studies.

Fourth, it would be very nice if the building had new paint. *This change* would make the building more attractive, *give* new students a more positive first impression of the school, *and reflect* the excellent education that students can get here.

I hope that these suggestions will receive your approval. These suggestions will *not only* improve student life at the English Language Institute *but also* help to attract new students. / *These suggestions will both* improve student life at the English Language Institute *and* help to attract new students.

8d   Overuse of *and, but,* and *so,* page 31

Answers will vary. Sample answers:

. . . At the time of our marriage, we were still university students. *Our* parents advised us to wait until graduation to get married, but we did not want to wait *and* ignored our parents' advice. As a result, in the early years of our marriage, we had many problems.

Both of us had lived at home until our marriage, so we did not have any experience living independently. *We* did not know how to shop or cook or clean or make decisions for ourselves. *Although* our parents agreed to continue paying for our education, we had to pay for our apartment and food. *Therefore,* both of us had to get part-time jobs. *We* were exhausted all the time, and we had many arguments.

Many couples in our situation would have gotten divorced. *However,* we were lucky, and we stayed together in spite of our problems. Both of us graduated from the university and got good jobs. *Once* we had more time and more money, *we* didn't argue so much, and we really began to enjoy our lives together. Now we are expecting our first baby, and we feel very happy and grateful for our good fortune.

9b   Inverted (verb-subject) word order, pages 32–33

A. 1. The little girl *quickly opened* her birthday presents. / The little girl *opened her birthday presents quickly.*
2. *Had I* studied harder in high school, I might have been accepted at a better university.
3. After graduating from college, my best friend and I traveled *in Europe and North Africa for three months.*
4. Rarely *does Blanca drink* more than one cup of coffee per day.
5. How long *have you lived* in Canada?

Copyright © 2003 by Pearson Education, Inc.

6. While working in the back of the house, I heard my doorbell ring. I went to open the door. *On the front porch stood* a delivery man holding an enormous box. "Are you Rosemary Baxter?" *he asked.* "No," I replied. *"She lives next door."*

B. 1. There are new students in my class nearly every week.
   2. Seldom do tourists visit our small town in the winter.
   3. Should you need any help, please do not hesitate to ask.
   4. How long has India been an independent country?
   5. It is difficult for me to get up early in the morning.
   6. We often eat breakfast in bed on weekends.

9c **Word order of direct and indirect objects, pages 34–35**

A. 1. Could you please make a cup of tea *for me?*
   2. As soon as I walked into the house, my husband handed an important-looking letter *to me.*
   3. Every year on my birthday, my mother cooks all my favorite dishes *for me.*
   4. Could you do a big favor *for me?* Would you mind lending your car *to me?*
   5. While I was away at college, my boyfriend sent an e-mail message *to me* every day.
   6. If you're going to the supermarket, could you please get some milk *for me?*
   7. George, who is an excellent carpenter, built a treehouse in the backyard *for his daughter.*
   8. Mr. Chin got a new suit *for himself* when he was in London.
   9. My boss asked me to show the report *to her* before I mailed it to the customer.
   10. If the product you buy is defective, most stores will refund your money *to you.*

B. Last night my roommate introduced one of her classmates *to me.* She said his name *to me,* but I couldn't hear it. "What?" I asked. Then my roommate pronounced his name *for me,* but I still couldn't get it.

"Could you repeat it again *for me?*" I asked.
"Sure. It's Jedidiah. But you can just call me Jed, OK?"
"OK," I replied. "What does your name mean? Can you translate it *for me?*"
"It means 'Friend of God' in the Hebrew language."
"That's beautiful," I replied. "Thank you for explaining your name *to me.*"

9d **Varying sentence openings, page 36**

. . .

My family lives in New York City, and we own a beach house on Long Island. We spend a month there every summer, swimming, fishing, and just hanging out on the beach. My cousins were visiting seven years ago, and one day we decided to try something we had seen in a movie. *First,* we found an empty wine bottle. *After that,* we took a piece of paper, and we wrote down our names, addresses, and ages. I wrote an additional message since I was the oldest, asking the person who found the bottle to please call me either on Long Island or in New York.

Then my cousins and I sailed out into the Atlantic Ocean and dropped the bottle in the water about two miles from the shore. *Wondering when and by whom it would be found,* we watched it drift away slowly.

We searched the beach every morning from then until the end of our vacation to see if the bottle had miraculously returned during the night. Of course it did not. Summer ended, we returned to the city, school began, and eventually we forgot all about the bottle.

One evening about two years later, I was doing my homework when the telephone rang. I picked it up absentmindedly and said, "Hello?" A woman's voice replied "'Allo? You are Max Waller?" She had a clear French accent. *Yes, I said,* I was Max Waller. She said she had found a bottle on the beach containing my name and address and a request to call. She then said the most astonishing thing of all: She had a son whose name was also Max, who was just about my age, and he was learning English in school.

I had just started taking French in school, amazingly. The other Max and I spoke a few words on the phone and exchanged e-mail addresses. We became penpals in this way. *For*

Copyright © 2003 by Pearson Education, Inc.

the next five years, we wrote to each other regularly. From time to time, we also spoke on the phone.

This summer, five years later, Max and I are finally going to meet. Both of us are going to graduate from high school this June, and our parents are going to give us the same gift: the opportunity to visit each other in our home countries. *On June 20* Max will come here from France and stay with my family at the beach for one month. *After that* I will return to France with him for a month.

In the fall both of us are going to start our university studies. Can you guess what each of us plans to study? I, predictably, am going to major in French. And Max is going to major in . . . economics!

10b-c Informal language and slang / Gender-sensitive (sexist) language, pages 37–38

1. Cindy, please put this letter outside in the mailbox so that the *mail carrier / letter carrier / postal worker* can pick it up tomorrow.
2. Answers will vary. Sample answer: "Please *pay attention* because it's time for us to *start.*"
3. Peter's *mother* is a dentist, and his *father* is a photographer.
4. I was very thirsty, so I asked the *flight attendant* to bring me a glass of orange juice.
5. If *you want* to be a *police officer, you* must graduate from the police academy and spend two years under the direct supervision of an *experienced police officer.* (OR If *people want* to become *police officers, they* must graduate from the police academy and spend two years under the direct supervision of an experienced *police officer.*)
6. Student: *Sir / Ma'am / Mr. X / Ms. X / Mrs. X / Professor X / Dr. X,* can I make an appointment to talk to you after school?
   Teacher: What do you want to talk about?
   Student: Well, I *failed / did poorly on* the last math exam.
   Teacher: I *understand.* All right, why don't you come to my office at 3:15?
7. In the United States, kindergarten *teachers* must have a college education. *They are* also required to do at least one year of supervised teaching before *they* can teach a class by *themselves.*

8. These days security at airports is very strict. Therefore, *all airline passengers have to have their* bags checked before *they are* allowed to enter the boarding area.
9. Most *waiters / restaurant workers / food servers* earn only about $5.00 an hour. They depend on tips from their customers to make a decent living.

PART 3   Grammar

11b   Verb tenses, pages 39–46

PRACTICE 1

1. am sitting	12. is closely
2. am watching	watching
3. are having	13. is
4. has	14. is whispering
5. looks	15. appears
6. is drinking	16. are they doing
7. saying	17. are getting up
8. has	18. walking
9. is	19. has
10. is not paying	20. is running
11. is saying	21. calling

PRACTICE 2

A. 1. have been sighting / have sighted
   2. has been increasing / has increased
   3. have been working / have worked
   4. have been pouring / have poured
   5. have reported / have been reporting
   6. have been investigating
   7. haven't been able
   8. have been preparing
   9. haven't completed
   10. have solved
   11. have investigated
   12. have had

B. 1. Jack has always *loved* music.
   2. He has been taking piano lessons *for* four years.
   3. This year he *has* gone to three classical performances.
   4. He has also *attended* several rock and pop concerts.
   5. He has never *gone* to a jazz concert, however.

PRACTICE 3

A. 1. called, didn't answer, was attending, left
   2. happened, was yawning, flew, swallowed
   3. was lying, reading, heard, got up, looked, were cutting

Copyright © 2003 by Pearson Education, Inc.

B. 1. has been planning
2. got
3. has been helping
4. haven't had
5. hasn't found
6. have visited
7. told
8. responded
9. have never enjoyed

PRACTICE 4

A. 1. had just washed, began
2. was, had lost, didn't know
3. started, had already had, had worked

B. 1. had been waiting, arrived, apologized, explained, had been, had been waiting, hit, wasn't
2. has been snowing
3. was snowing, heard, had been snowing
4. had lived / had been living, came, hadn't received, was, told, had been, had recovered, left

PRACTICE 5

A. 2. will be able
3. will kill / will have killed
4. will have been traveling
5. will grow / will have grown

B. 2. will have lost
3. will have been married
4. will have been studying

C. 1. will be / are going to be
2. is going to / will
3. will start / is going to start / is starting
4. are going / are going to go
5. will you be living / are you going to be living
6. is leaving / leaves / is going to leave

PRACTICE 6

. . . Two women, one of whom was pregnant, were sitting at a table near me, and they were talking about baby names. The not-pregnant one asked if the pregnant one and her husband *had* chosen names for the baby yet. The pregnant one replied, "Well, if it's a boy, my husband wants to call him Robert Junior."

I didn't understand her answer. I *learned* / *had learned* in school that *junior* means "lower in rank." I *wondered* why anyone would give this name to a baby. In my country, China, we prefer names with a positive meaning.

I *went* home and *looked* up *junior* in the dictionary. It *explained* that in the United States, some families put the word *junior* after a boy's name if he has the same first name as his father. This helped me to understand what the pregnant woman *said.* Also, now I *understand* why two American presidents have the same name. George Bush was the forty-first president of the United States, and George Bush *Junior,* his son, was the forty-third.

11c Special tense combinations, pages 47–55

PRACTICE 1

1. started, has changed
2. got, went
3. has changed, began, owned
4. have become, joined, have spent
5. finish, go
6. closes, am going to meet / am meeting
7. eat, are going to go / are going
8. won't go, rises, get, will eat, will sleep

PRACTICE 2

A. 1. don't hurry
2. are going to miss / will miss
3. had put
4. wouldn't need
5. miss
6. am not driving / won't drive
7. will be
8. have to walk
9. will / would
10. have / had

B. 1. If I *were* a U.S. citizen, I would not need a visa to study at an American university.
2. Had I *known* it was going to rain, I would have taken an umbrella.
3. If Gina had gotten a higher score on the university entrance exam, she could have *gone* to Harvard University.
4. If I *had* a better job, I could afford to buy a house instead of renting an apartment.
5. (*Correct*)
6. If you had to learn another language, which one *would* you choose?
7. I would have joined the swimming team if I had *had* more time.

Copyright © 2003 by Pearson Education, Inc.

PRACTICE 3

1. unless	6. in case
2. Provided (that)/ As long as	7. In the event (that), In case
3. unless	8. In the event (that), In case
4. in case, in the event (that)	
5. As long as, Provided (that)	

PRACTICE 4

1. Nancy asked Ellen where she had met him.
2. Ellen answered that she had met him while she was standing in line at the supermarket the night before.
3. Ellen added that he was (had been) nice looking and very charming.
4. Nancy inquired if (whether) they had exchanged phone numbers.
5. Ellen replied that he had given her his number and (had) asked her to call him the next day.
6. Nancy wanted to know if Ellen was going to go out with him.
7. Ellen said she wished she could, but she couldn't.
8. Nancy asked why.
9. Ellen explained that he had a dog and that she was allergic to dogs.
10. Nancy concluded that in that case, maybe *she* should go out with him.

PRACTICE 5

A.
1. turn in
2. be
3. follow
4. study, discuss
5. meet

B.
1. It is necessary that you pay your phone bill on time.
2. It is urgent that we call the fire department if we smell gas.
3. It is vital that American workers pay their income taxes by April 15.
4. It is advisable that a person see a doctor if she hits her head.
5. It is important that I buy my textbook before the next class.

PRACTICE 6

1. sew	7. take
2. be	8. perform
3. (to) prepare	9. (to) do, taken
4. arrange	10. served, dance,
5. to decorate	enjoy
6. done	

11d Modals, pages 56–59

PRACTICE 1

. . . As a result, many Swiss people *can speak* several languages.

In recent years, English has become increasingly popular in Switzerland. Thousands of tourists visit Switzerland each year, and most of them *can't speak* any of the country's official languages. Almost all of them *can speak* English, however.

Some Swiss people are worried about the growing use of English in their country. They ask: "What effect *will / might* the use of English have on the relationships between the different linguistic groups in the country?" These people are afraid that English *may take* over as the principal method of communication in the country and that this *could cause* the minor languages to die out. They say that the Swiss people *must not allow* this to happen because multilingualism is an essential feature of Swiss history, culture, and identity.

PRACTICE 2

1. would rather
2. should / ought to / had better / has to / must
3. May / Can / Could
4. have to / must, don't have to
5. must
6. can't / couldn't
7. should / ought to / had better / have to / must
8. can't, Would . . . mind
9. had to

PRACTICE 3

1. must have overslept
2. could have taken, could have called
3. must have had
4. should have bought
5. shouldn't have eaten
6. would rather have stayed, should have stayed
7. may / might / must not have finished
8. couldn't have gone
9. could / might / must have been
10. wouldn't have made

11e Passive voice, pages 60–62

PRACTICE 1

A.
1. Every four or five years, the law office where I work is remodeled.
2. It is being remodeled now.

Copyright © 2003 by Pearson Education, Inc.

3. An interior decorator was hired by the office manager to plan and manage the work.
4. The physical labor is being done by a crew of workers.
5. By the time I arrived this morning, the old carpeting had been removed.
6. The manager's office was being painted.
7. The new furniture will be delivered later this week.
8. The whole job will have been finished by the end of the week.
9. (*Not possible to change.*)

B. 1. was bitten
  2. was picked up
  3. reported
  4. was identified
  5. is/was frequently chased
  6. wanted
  7. was charged
  8. is suing

PRACTICE 2
A. . . . As soon as he walked in the door, he could see that his apartment had been robbed. His computer had been taken. His closets had been searched, and his clothes had been dumped on the floor. A valuable painting was missing. Worst of all, his sweet old cat was dead. Apparently, she had been poisoned by the robber.

B. The Hebrew alphabet is written from left to right. Vowels are omitted in most printed materials. When vowels are used, they are placed under the words. The first letter of the Hebrew alphabet is called *alef.* The second letter is called *bet.* This is the origin of the word *alphabet,* which is used in many European languages. The Hebrew writing system was invented many thousands of years ago. The Hebrew Bible (which is called the Old Testament by Christians) was written in Hebrew. However, the New Testament was written in a language called Aramaic. Aramaic was spoken by the common people in Palestine at the time of Jesus. Later, the New Testament was translated from Aramaic into Greek. Most of the translations that are used today are based on the early Greek one.

12a **Gerunds, pages 63–68**

PRACTICE 1
A. 1. Playing with balls and blocks helps babies learn how to hold and manipulate objects.
  2. Listening to stories develops young children's listening and speaking skills.
  3. Holding a pencil and drawing gets kindergarten children ready for writing.

B. 1. I enjoy/don't enjoy reading the newspaper in the morning.
  2. I enjoy/don't enjoy seeing action films.
  3. I enjoy/don't enjoy playing with animals.
  4. I enjoy/don't enjoy spending time with young children.
  5. I enjoy/don't enjoy sleeping outdoors.

C. 1. having done
  2. having copied
  3. cheating
  4. studying

PRACTICE 2
1. a. to raising
  b. of singing
  c. about accepting
  d. against taking
  e. about being
2. f. on giving
  g. of/about having
  h. to finishing
3. i. on studying
  j. from being
  k. for making

PRACTICE 3
  2. to having
  3. of being
  4. about living
  5. about having
  6. to do
  7. to doing
  8. to taking
  9. to cooking
  10. to living
  11. for making

PRACTICE 4
A. Answers will vary.
B. 1. taking pictures
  2. arguing
  3. shining, blowing
  4. playing, reaching
C. 1. drawing
  2. opening
  3. sharing
  4. getting
  5. playing

Copyright © 2003 by Pearson Education, Inc.

12b Infinitives, pages 69–76

PRACTICE 1

1. to carry
2. to be signed
3. to study
4. to tune
5. to be picked up, held
6. to meet / to have met
7. to have grown
8. to live / to be living
9. to drive
10. to be promoted

PRACTICE 2

1. It is courteous for people to remove their shoes when entering a Japanese home.
2. In many countries, it is polite for guests to make noises while eating because it shows that the food is tasty.
3. In the United States, it is very rude to point at someone with your middle finger.
4. It was fascinating for me to taste new foods when I visited Indonesia.
5. It often feels strange for students who come to study in the United States to call teachers by their first names.
6. It is necessary for speakers to make eye contact in some cultures.
7. In other cultures, it is preferable to avoid eye contact as a way of showing respect.
8. It was surprising for me to learn that in some cultures, white is the color of death.
9. It is foolish for drivers to offer a bribe to a police officer in North America.
10. It is useful to ask questions when you are in a new place.

PRACTICE 3

Answers will vary.

PRACTICE 4

A. 1. Q: Would you feel lucky to find a four-leaf clover?
   A: Yes, I would feel lucky to find a four-leaf clover. / No, I would not feel lucky to find a four-leaf clover.
2. Q: Would you feel horrified to break a mirror?
   A: Yes, I would feel horrified to break a mirror. / No, I would not feel horrified to break a mirror.
3. Q: Would you be afraid to go out on Friday the thirteenth?
   A: Yes, I would be afraid to go out on Friday the thirteenth. / No, I would not be afraid to go out on Friday the thirteenth.

4. Q: Would you feel fortunate to see a shooting star?
   A: Yes, I would feel fortunate to see a shooting star. / No, I would not feel fortunate to see a shooting star.
5. Q: Would you be careful not to walk under a ladder?
   A: Yes, I would be careful not to walk under a ladder. / No, I would not be careful not to walk under a ladder.

B. 1. In 1926, Floyd Bennet and Robert Byrd were the first people to fly over the North Pole.
2. In 1927, Charles Lindbergh was the first person to fly nonstop across the Atlantic Ocean alone.
3. In 1932, Amelia Earhart was the first woman to repeat Lindbergh's accomplishment.

C. 1. Computers can be used to order groceries.
2. Electric mixers can be used to prepare cakes.
3. Microwave ovens can be used to cook meals.
4. Robots can be used to vacuum the house.

PRACTICE 5

A. 1. too young
2. very mature
3. old enough
4. old enough
5. very responsible
6. experienced enough
7. very hard

B. 1. too weak to see the traffic signs.
2. good enough to hear emergency vehicles.
3. not quick enough to react quickly.
4. too stubborn to give up driving.

12c Gerunds vs. infinitives, pages 77–78

1. packing / to pack; to pack
2. waiting / to wait
3. to talk
4. to stay / staying
5. to check
6. to check
7. to enter
8. to take off
9. to bargain
10. to get
11. being
12. thinking

Copyright © 2003 by Pearson Education, Inc.

12d   Phrasal verbs, pages 79–80

1. take off,
   keep . . . on
2. dress up
3. try . . . on
4. drop in
5. throw out / throw
   away, stay up, get
   together
6. show up
7. stand up
8. passes away
9. take . . . back

13   Subject-Verb Agreement, page 81

1. were
2. is
3. is
4. is / are
5. speak
6. stays
7. are
8. is
9. make
10. are
11. is
12. is
13. is / are
14. are
15. comes
16. work, are
17. Is
18. makes
19. grows

14a–c   Nouns: Count and noncount, pages 82–83

1. work
2. a fire
3. some stuff
4. some mail
5. some junk
6. some garbage
7. time
8. some soccer
9. television
10. food
11. Coffee
12. milk
13. some ice cream
14. some lettuce
15. mayonnaise
16. dinner
17. chicken
18. some spinach
19. cheese
20. fruit
21. luggage

14d   Expressing quantity, page 84

Recently I took up a new hobby: gardening. I began by reading (~~one~~, a couple of, a few, ~~a little~~) books about it, and I talked to (a number of, ~~few of~~, some of) friends who are experienced gardeners. I don't have (much, ~~many~~, a lot of, ~~some~~) spare time, so my friends recommended (~~every~~, ~~a little~~, a few, ~~any~~) plants that would look nice and wouldn't require (much, ~~many~~, ~~several~~, ~~a little~~) care.

After that, I paid my first visit to a gardening store. I spent (~~both~~, a couple of, a number of, ~~any~~) hours talking to the workers and looking at plants. There were (~~much~~, many, ~~few~~, a lot of) varieties, and I had a difficult time choosing what to buy. I wish I could have bought (every, each, ~~both~~, ~~all~~) plant in the store! In the end, though, I selected (a couple of, a number of, ~~a great deal of~~, a few) small bushes, (several, ~~a little~~, ~~every~~, five) types of flowers, and (some, several, ~~much~~, ~~a great deal of~~) packages of vegetable seeds. I also bought (some, ~~one~~, a few, many) tools and (a lot of, a great deal of, ~~much~~, ~~many~~) fertilizer because the earth in my garden is not very rich.

It took me a couple of weeks to plant everything. Now, (several, a few, ~~both~~, ~~much~~) months later, the plants are blooming and the vegetables are growing. It doesn't require (much, ~~many~~, a lot of, ~~plenty of~~) effort to keep the garden going. I spend (~~an~~, a few, several, ~~some~~) hours working there (each, every, ~~several~~, all) weekend and I make sure to give the plants (lots of, plenty of, ~~much~~, ~~most~~) water. I get (a great deal of, plenty of, lots of, ~~a couple of~~) pleasure from my beautiful garden.

15a   Articles for generic nouns: a, an, or no article (Ø), page 85

1. G, NG
2. G
3. G, NG
4. NG, G
5. G, NG
6. G
7. NG
8. NG

15c   Articles for definite nouns: the, page 86

Correct articles:

1. an
2. some
3. The
4. The
5. the
6. the
7. a
8. the
9. the
10. the
11. the
12. the
13. a
14. the
15. the
16. the
17. the
18. the
19. the

15   Articles, pages 87–88

A.
1. Ø
2. the
3. the
4. Ø
5. the
6. the
7. the
8. Ø
9. the
10. Ø
11. the
12. the

B.
1. The
2. the
3. the
4. the
5. Ø
6. The
7. the
8. Ø
9. the
10. a
11. The
12. a
13. the
14. Ø
15. the
16. the
17. the
18. a

Copyright © 2003 by Pearson Education, Inc.

C. 1. a   **4.** an   **7.** ∅
    2. ∅   **5.** ∅   **8.** ∅
    3. the   **6.** ∅   **9.** the

16a–b Subject, object, and possessive pronouns/Special situations, pages 89–90

A. 1. whose, who, his
2. he, his, they
3. its, which
4. whom, her, they

B. 1. I
2. she
3. I
4. whom
5. whose
6. mine, who
7. our

16c–d *Myself, ourselves/ Each other and one another,* page 91

A. 1. myself   **4.** myself
2. himself   **5.** themselves
3. themselves

B. When I was a child both my parents worked outside the house, so my four brothers and sisters and I sometimes stayed home by *ourselves.* It was not a problem for us to be alone because the older ones took care of the younger ones, and we all knew we could depend on *one another/each other.* Our parents always encouraged us to be independent. As a result, from a young age, I learned to solve problems by *myself.* Today I am a father too, and I also encourage my children to do as many things as possible for *themselves.*

17 Pronoun Agreement, page 92

1. . . . Upon arrival, each passenger is required to have *his or her* luggage checked. If someone is carrying a gun or any kind of sharp object, *he or she* will be questioned and possibly even arrested.

2. Passengers must pass through a metal detector and have their carry-on bags x-rayed. At this point, they must say good-bye to their family and friends because no one except passengers with tickets *is* allowed past the metal detectors.

3. Procedures for picking up arriving passengers have also changed. In the past, passengers could be met at the gate as soon as *they* got off the plane. Nowadays, *they* must be met in the baggage-claim area.

4. Last week my parents and my brother flew to London together. The security check before the flight took more than an hour. Luckily, neither my brother nor my parents were told to open *their* bags.

5. The new security measures are time-consuming and inconvenient. Nevertheless, most people cooperate with *them* because everybody understands that these measures could save *his or her life./ . . .* because *they understand that these measures could save their lives.*

18 Pronouns: Unclear Reference, page 93

1. . . . According to the new rules, any student caught cheating will fail the course in which the cheating occurred. If *the cheating* happens again, the student will be expelled from the university. Many students were upset about the *new measures.* They said that *the measures* weren't fair because under the new rules, a student's entire career could be destroyed by one "mistake."

2. My roommate was one of the first people punished under the new rules. His physics professor caught him cheating during a test. *The professor* saw *my roommate* looking at notes he had hidden in his sleeve. Because it was *my roommate's* first offense, he got an F, and he will have to repeat *the course* in summer school. When I asked him why he had cheated instead of studying a little harder, his excuse was "Everyone does it."

19 Adjectives and adverbs, Position, page 94

Wife: Well, dinner is *almost ready.*
Husband: What can I do to help? Do you want me to make the salad?
Wife: I made *the salad this morning.* Let's see. . . . We're having *chicken soup.* I made it last night, so we need to heat it. Could you take it out of the refrigerator and put it on the stove? Lift *the pot carefully;* it's heavy.
Husband: OK. What else?
Wife: Check the table. I can't remember if I put out soup spoons.
Husband: *I've already* done it.

Copyright © 2003 by Pearson Education, Inc.

An hour later.

Wife: I'm getting worried about your parents. They're *half an hour late.* It's *the first time* they've *ever been late.* Why haven't they called us?

Husband: I don't know. They're *probably stuck in traffic.* But if they don't arrive soon, I'm going to call the police.

20b Order of adjectives, page 95

My family originates from Greece, so when my cousin got married last week, she had a *traditional Greek Orthodox church ceremony.* She wore *an old-fashioned cream silk gown* with a *long lace* train, and she carried a bouquet of red, yellow, and white flowers. The groom, who also comes from a *very large Greek family,* wore a *formal gray* suit.

The afternoon wedding was followed by a very loud, festive party in the evening. The guests talked, laughed, sang, danced, and ate huge quantities of *delicious Greek* food. There was a *fantastic band* that played *both traditional and modern music.* I loved seeing my *tiny old* grandmother dancing with the slightly embarrassed groom.

My cousin received many wonderful wedding gifts. However, she told me that her favorite gift was a pair of *antique silver* candlesticks that she got from our grandmother.

20c Participial adjectives: *boring or bored?* pages 96–97

1. embarrassed
2. relaxing, satisfying
3. terrifying, frightened, thrilling
4. depressed, confusing
5. irritating
6. exhausted

21 Comparisons, pages 98–99

2. the smoothest
3. the least noisy
4. the most enjoyable
5. roomier than
6. the most expensive
7. as many points as
8. as comfortable
9. as safe as
10. better gas mileage
11. less expensive
12. as many optional features as
13. quieter than
14. as quiet as
15. less comfortable than
16. the least attractive
17. the least expensive
18. as well as
19. the most popular

22 Negatives, page 100

1. Now he makes a lot of money, but he is *not* happy.
2. He has to leave the house at 6:30 a.m., so he is *not* home when his children wake up in the morning.
3. He *doesn't* come home until 7:00 or 8:00 in the evening.
4. He *can't* eat dinner with his family.
5. He *barely* has time to see his children before they go to bed.
6. In the evenings, he has *no* energy to do *anything* except watch television.
7. His wife complains, "You *never* talk to me *anymore.*" / "You *don't ever* talk to me *anymore.*"
8. Mr. Connolly regrets taking the new job. It's nice to have more money, but after all, money is *not* everything.

23 Adjective Clauses, pages 101–102

A. 1. There is something I want *to say to you,* so listen carefully.
   2. My father's mother, *whose house is near the beach,* swims in the ocean every day.
   3. In Chinatown, there are thousands of Chinese people who *don't* speak English.
   4. I have a very strange neighbor *who lives by herself and never talks to anybody.*
   5. *Our teacher, who has a wonderful sense of humor,* told us a hilarious story.
   6. W. A. Mozart was born in *Salzburg, a famous center for music.* / W. A. Mozart was born in Austria, *which was a famous center for music.*

B. 1. The students *whose names were called* raised their hands.
   2. The girl *who/that explained the homework to me* was very helpful.
   3. On our trip, we visited many areas of the United States (*that/which*) we had *never seen before.*
   4. The place (*which/that*) *we are taking you to* is a secret.
   5. The woman *with whom I was dancing* stepped on my toe. / The woman *whom I was dancing with* stepped on my toe. / The woman I *was dancing with* stepped on my toe.
   6. Early morning is the time (*when*) *I do my best work.*
   7. The student *whose parents you just met* is in one of my classes.

Copyright © 2003 by Pearson Education, Inc.

PART 4   Punctuation

24   End punctuation, page 103

1. My husband said he wanted to take me out to dinner.
2. He asked me which restaurant I wanted to go to.
3. I thought about it for a while.
4. What kind of food did I feel like having? Mexican? French? Indian? Persian?
5. Finally I chose a French restaurant that some friends had recommended.
6. My husband made a reservation for 7:00 p.m.
7. However, without my knowledge, he made some other plans as well.
8. When we arrived at the restaurant, we were escorted to a private room.
9. As we walked in, I saw about fifteen of our friends sitting there.
10. "Surprise!" they shouted.

25a   Commas in compound sentences, page 104

1. Living downtown has both advantages and disadvantages.
2. My office is downtown, so I can walk to work most of the time.
3. I enjoy being close to theaters and museums.
4. Shopping is very convenient, and there are many excellent restaurants nearby.
5. On the other hand, I don't like the traffic or the noise of the big city.
6. My friends complain that it is difficult to find parking near my apartment.
7. My family does not live near me, so I sometimes feel isolated and lonely.
8. Now I am single, so I think the advantages of living downtown are greater than the disadvantages.
9. (*Correct*)

25b   Commas after introducers, page 105

2. (*Correct*)
3. (*Correct*)
4. (*Correct*)
5. Almost immediately, she stops working and starts to daydream about the party on Saturday night.
6. Another interruption comes when the phone rings.

7. While she is talking on the phone, the water on the stove boils.
8. As quickly as possible, she ends the conversation, goes to the kitchen, and prepares the coffee.
9. Carrying the cup of coffee, she returns to her desk once again.
10. Before long, she looks at the clock and realizes it is time to watch her favorite program on television.
11. In the end, Ms. Baker decides that the lessons will have to wait until later.

25c   Commas around extra-information modifiers, pages 106–107

A. 1. **b:** Mr. Jones, who lives next door, has six daughters.
2. **a:** Our town's biggest law firm recently hired a new lawyer. The lawyer, who went to Harvard Law School, will no doubt receive an excellent salary.
3. **b:** My secretary, running to board the train, slipped on the platform, fell, and broke her arm.
4. **a:** The president of the United States has two homes. The primary residence, located in Washington, D.C., is the White House.
5. **a:** Strawberries, which grow in warm weather, are not available during the winter.
6. **a:** My sister, Joyce, lives in San Diego.

B. 1. My oldest brother, Kenneth, is married to my wife's sister.
2. Children learning to speak two languages at the same time do not mix languages very often.
3. Many countries that have a king or a queen also have a prime minister or president.
4. Vitamin D, which aids in bone and tooth formation, can be toxic in very large amounts.
5. After winning $50,000 in the lottery, my uncle bought a beautiful house located on the shore of a lake.

25d   Commas with transition signals, page 108

2. . . . On the other hand, the Chinese alligator, which is smaller than its American cousin, is nearly extinct.

Copyright © 2003 by Pearson Education, Inc.

3. . . . For example, many people believe that they can live for hundreds of years. This is untrue, however; in fact, wild alligators live to be 30 or 40 years old, while captive alligators may live 60 to 80 years.
4. . . . However, they can live only in warm, wet climates. Therefore, there are no crocodiles in Canada, northern Europe, or Russia.
5. . . . In fact, only about 500 wild crocodiles remain on the whole continent. For that reason, crocodiles are considered to be an endangered species and are protected by law.

25e–f   Commas with direct quotations/Commas with items in a series, page 109

1. (*Correct*)
2. "Tired, hungry, stressed, and overworked," the daughter replied. "I can't wait for the weekend."
3. The mother inquired, "Do you have much homework tonight?"
4. "Some," said the daughter. "I have to finish a book report and study for a huge Spanish test."
5. "Mrs. Carlin called and asked if you can babysit Friday evening," the mother said.
6. "No way," the daughter answered. "This Friday night I'm staying home, watching TV, and going to bed early."
7. "You said that you wanted to babysit every week, earn money, and go shopping at the end of the month," the mother said.
8. "I know," the daughter said, "but I can babysit next Friday and Saturday."

25g   Other uses of commas, page 110

A.

CREDIT CARD APPLICATION	
Name (last, first):	*Tanaka, Hiroshi*
Date of birth:	*May 7, 1975*
Place of birth:	*Kobe, Japan*
Address:	*3482 Rodeo Drive, Beverly Hills, California 90210*
Occupation:	*Investment banker*
Annual salary:	*$175,000*

B.

Dear Daddy,

I went to the mall with Juni and didn't have time to walk the dog. Could you do it, please? I promise to do it tomorrow and the next day. Oh, I also promise to wash your car like I said I would.

Thanks, Dad. I'll be back around 10.

Love & kisses,

Lisa

26   Semicolons, page 111

A. 1. My living room is furnished with a carpet that I bought in Turkey, a leather sofa and armchair inherited from my grandmother, a wonderful floor lamp found at a garage sale, and photos of four generations of my family.
2. The room reflects a variety of styles; for example, the couch is contemporary, but one of the paintings is more than 100 years old.
3. My piano was imported from Germany; my bookcases were handmade by my uncle.

B. Answers will vary. Sample answers:

On Friday night my roommate and I went to a movie, and we returned to our apartment around 11:00 p.m. As we approached our front door, we could tell something was wrong because the front door was open. Entering cautiously, we immediately saw that the place had been burglarized. In the living room all our books and CDs lay scattered on the floor, the furniture had been overturned, there was glass everywhere, and the television was gone. We went next door and called the police immediately. However, they did not arrive until two hours later.

Copyright © 2003 by Pearson Education, Inc.

27   Colons, page 112

1. Please bring the following items to every class: a pencil or pen, an eraser, lined paper, your textbook, and a dictionary.
2. Your essay has two qualities that I admire: excellent writing and thought-provoking ideas.
3. My father's favorite saying was the following: "It is better to keep your mouth shut and be thought a fool than to open it and remove all doubt."
4. When I go to college, I plan to major in engineering, computer science, or physics.
5. My grandmother, who became a widow at an early age, had two prized possessions: her wedding ring and a love letter from her husband.
6. My favorite nineteenth-century American authors are Mark Twain and Walt Whitman.
7. Last night we rented the movie *Austin Powers: The Spy Who Shagged Me.*
8. We always take a break at 2:50 p.m.
9. The colors of the Italian flag are green, white, and red.
10. This cake has only six ingredients: flour, sugar, eggs, oil, baking powder, and salt.

28a   Apostrophes with possessives, page 113

1. the earth's diameter
2. the mountains' height
3. the table's surface
4. the chairs' legs
5. the mother and father's room
6. the children's play area
7. my sister-in-law's mother
8. Mrs. Allen's and Mrs. Ellis's schedules
9. the queen of England's home
10. the politicians' speeches
11. the UN's policy
12. nobody's responsibility

28   Apostrophes, page 114

1. It's a beautiful day.
2. The angry man's car was towed because he had parked in a no-parking zone.
3. My daughter's two best friends' birthdays are on the same day.
4. Yesterday I bought three CDs and spent the evening listening to music.

5. I received a catalogue advertising men's shoes.
6. The government reaffirmed its policy to provide free education for all citizens.
7. Last Friday we were invited to the Thomases'.
8. Tonight we're having dinner at the Bakers'.
9. Her handwriting is unclear. I can't tell the difference between her M's and N's.
10. Feeling lonely, Agnes ate a whole box of chocolates by herself.
11. If you don't proofread your essay, it's going to be full of spelling mistakes.
12. **A:** Where's your math book?
    B: I don't know. Can I borrow yours?

29   Quotation Marks, page 115

2. "What do you think their bark sounds like?" I asked him.
3. "It depends," he said. "If the dog is big, I think it sounds like *woof-woof.* But little dogs sound like they're saying 'arf-arf.'"
4. "Did you know," I responded, "that people around the world imitate animals' sounds in different ways?"
5. "Huh?" he replied.
6. I explained, "For example, in Spanish, dogs say 'guau guau.' In Hebrew it's 'hav hav,' and in Japanese, it's 'wan wan' or 'kyan kyan.'"
7. "But don't animals make the same sounds everywhere?" he asked, puzzled.
8. "Of course they do," I answered. "But speakers of different languages express the sounds differently."
9. "That's so funny!" my son exclaimed. "Where'd you hear about this?"
10. "On a radio program called 'Pet Talk'; I heard it in the car on my way to work."

30–31   Parentheses/Dashes, page 116

1. The procedure for guessing unfamiliar words is as follows: (a) read the whole sentence in which the word appears; (b) determine the part of speech of the unfamiliar word; (c) look in the sentence for clues to the meaning; (d) think of a word or phrase that fits in the sentence instead of the unfamiliar word.
2. Abraham Lincoln (1809–1865) was the sixteenth president of the United States.

Copyright © 2003 by Pearson Education, Inc.

3. We spent all day Saturday—from 8:00 a.m. to 6:00 p.m.—working in the garden.
4. Jerusalem is a holy city to three major religions—Judaism, Christianity, and Islam.
5. The famous actor owned a Porsche, a Mercedes, a Jaguar, a Ferrari, and a 1968 Volkswagen Beetle—a gift from his father when he was eighteen years old.
6. Danny—Please remember to put the dog outside before you leave. Make sure there's water in his bowl.
7. Some fruits—peaches, avocados, plums, apricots—will ripen faster if you keep them inside a paper bag.

PART 5   Mechanics

33 Capital Letters, pages 117–118

1. Karen Andres is the student advisor at the English Language Institute.

2. Dear Ms. Andres:
Last Friday I dropped off my resume, but unfortunately it contained an error. Here is a corrected copy. Could you please remove the old one from my file and replace it with this one? Thank you.
Yours truly,
Lorena Cardozo

3.

Résumé	
Lorena Cardozo	
401 Second Avenue	
Hollywood, California 90049	
Desired Position:	Teaching intern, Oak Elementary School
Education:	University of California, Riverside: MA, Education, 2004 (expected) California State University, Northridge: BA, Spanish, 2002
Teaching Experience:	Teaching assistant, Psychology 101, fall semester 2003 Spanish language tutor, 1998 to present
Other Experience:	Intern at Los Angeles Times newspaper, summer 2001 Volunteer at Daycare Center, Kraft Corp., 1999 Camp counselor, Roxbury Park, summer 1996–1998
Additional Skills:	Languages: Spanish, French (fluent), Arabic (beginner) Music: I play the guitar and sing.
Travel:	North America, Western Europe, and the Middle East
Interests:	Renaissance art and music; folk dancing; ethnic cooking
References:	Available from University Career Center California State University, Northridge 18233 Norton Avenue Northridge, CA 91330

34 Hyphens, page 119

1. My sister-in-law is studying for a Ph.D. in literature. Her dissertation deals with postmodern poetry.
2. Being criticized in front of others can be damaging to a child's self-esteem.
3. My brother and his ex-wife still talk to each other almost every day.
4. (*Correct*)
5. Doctors and dentists advise pregnant women not to have Xrays taken.
6. My cousin was six feet tall by the time he was fourteen.
7. They bought a two-door car with four-wheel drive.
8. The cake recipe calls for three-fourths of a cup of butter.
9. Aren't you ashamed to turn in such a badly written essay?
10. The teacher gave the students a five-minute warning before instructing them to put down their pencils and hand in their exam papers.
11. One of the things I admire about movie director Steven Spielberg is his imagi-nation. (*or* do not hyphenate)
12. They have a good-tempered, sweet dog and an unfriendly, mean cat.

Copyright © 2003 by Pearson Education, Inc.

35 Underlining and Italics, page 120

1. One of the largest passenger ships ever built, the <u>Queen Mary</u> was purchased in 1967 by the city of Long Beach, California, where it is a popular tourist attraction.
2. The most profitable movie ever made was <u>Titanic</u>, which won eleven Academy Awards in 1998.
3. (*Correct*)
4. Mrs. Park keeps track of her students' test scores using an <u>Excel</u> spreadsheet.
5. The first time I saw the <u>Mona Lisa</u>, by Leonardo da Vinci, I was surprised that the famous painting was so small.
6. Every Christmas, the ballet <u>The Nutcracker</u>, by Peter Illich Tchaikovsky, is broadcast on American television.
7. (*Correct*)
8. The current issue of <u>National Geographic</u> online has an article called "Inside the Tornado" about a man who chases tornadoes to collect scientific data.
9. Americans are fond of self-help books. One of the earliest and most famous books was <u>How to Win Friends and Influence People</u>, by Dale Carnegie.
10. (*Correct*)

36 Abbreviations, page 121

1. In the fall she will be attending Johns Hopkins *University* in Baltimore, *Maryland,* where she plans to major in French *literature.*
2. Electric cars such as the EV1 can easily travel up to eighty *miles per hour.*
3. It will cost *approximately* $2 million to build a new wing on the *YMCA* building.
4. *Ms.* Estee Lauder, who was born in 1908, founded the famous cosmetics *corporation* of the same name during the Depression.
5. I hate getting up early, so this semester I have all my classes in the *afternoon/ evening.*
6. The sun is about 150 million *kilometers* from the earth.
7. Several senators had to wait two days for an *appointment* with the *president.*

8. *Dr.* Condoleeza Rice is National Security Affairs advisor to President George W. Bush.
9. During World War II, the Allied forces fighting against Germany consisted of the *United States,* the *United Kingdom,* and France.
10. My name is Soo-Jung Park, and I come from *Korea.* This year I am studying English in *Los Angeles, California,* in the United States of America.
11. (*Correct*)
12. (*Correct*)

37 Numbers, page 122

1. (*Correct*)
2. Tom Leppard, a retired soldier who lives in Scotland, has tattoos on ninety-nine *percent* of his body.
3. *Three* dogs have given birth to *twenty-three* puppies each.
4. The country with the largest population is China, with almost 1.3 *billion* people.
5. The world's deepest lake is Lake Baikal in Russia. It contains *one-fifth* of the world's fresh water.
6. The average Japanese man lives more than *seventy-seven* years, while the average woman lives nearly eighty-four years.
7. The world's largest religious group is the Roman Catholic Church, which has *17.4%* of the world's population.
8. All fourteen of the world's *8,000-meter* mountain peaks are in the Himalaya range.
9. The world's largest train station is Grand Central Terminal in New York City, built between *1903* and *1913.*
10. The first photographic image of the dark side of the moon was recorded at *6:30* a.m. on October 7, 1959, from a distance of *seven thousand* kilometers, by the Soviet spacecraft *Luna III.*

Copyright © 2003 by Pearson Education, Inc.

38a–c **Spelling, pages 123–124**

A. 1. latest
2. hopeless
3. ninth
4. tried
5. arriving
6. written
7. preferred

B. 1. tables
2. watches
3. dictionaries
4. toys
5. shelves
6. tomatoes
7. zeros / zeroes
8. women
9. people
10. sheep
11. pants
12. media
13. fathers-in-law
14. 1000s
15. BAs
16. M.D.s or M.D.'s
17. d's
18. statistics
19. altos
20. potatoes
21. stresses
22. news
23. calves
24. children

PART 6   Writing and Revising

40b **Organizing, pages 125–126**

Answers will vary. Sample answers:

II. Advantages
   A. Cultural opportunities
      3. opera
      4. libraries
   B. Educational opportunities
      2. public lectures on many subjects
   C. Job opportunities
III. Disadvantages
   A. Transportation
      3. expensive parking
   B. Expensive
      1. housing
      2. entertainment, e.g., movie tickets
   C. Impersonal
      2. shopkeepers and other service people don't care

40 **The Writing Process, pages 127–128**

Answers will vary. Sample answers:

A.   *Visiting San Francisco*

   San Francisco is *an outstanding vacation city for three reasons*. First, it has many famous tourist attractions such as the cable cars, Chinatown, Alcatraz Island, and Union Square. *More than 10 million tourists visit San Francisco each year, and some of these* attractions, such as Alcatraz, *are so popular that it is necessary to make reservations far ahead of time. A second reason for San Francisco's popularity with tourists is its world-famous restaurants,* which feature every imaginable type of ethnic food as well as outstanding fish dishes. Most meals in San Francisco are served with a unique type of bread called "sourdough." Though many people think it tastes strange at first, they soon develop a taste for it. ~~That's why many tourists leaving from San Francisco International Airport can be seen boarding their planes with a loaf of bread under their arm.~~ One more thing worth noting about San Francisco's restaurants is that they are known for their excellent service. The servers are courteous and professional, and patrons are treated like honored guests. ~~However, I ate at one restaurant in Chinatown where the service was terrible.~~ The third thing that makes San Francisco a great vacation city is its geographical situation. The city is small—only forty-nine square miles. The ocean surrounds it on three sides, and there are many hills. Consequently, beautiful views of the water and the downtown skyscrapers can be seen from many places in the city. In conclusion, you should visit San Francisco. *These are just three of many reasons why San Francisco is a popular vacation destination for people from all over the world.*

B.   **Traffic Problems in Seoul, Korea**

   Seoul, Korea, *has* one of highest traffic accident rates in the world; however, *it's* penalties for traffic violations and its automobile insurance rates are among the lowest. I believe that if the government increased the fines for traffic *violations*, fewer people would *cause* traffic problems. Furthermore, an increase in automobile insurance rates would make people think twice about owning a car. *Another* traffic regulation that could reduce the number of automobiles is one the government used during the Olympic Games in Seoul. It is a regulation whereby only certain automobiles can be on the road on a certain day according to their license plate numbers. For example, on Monday, Wednesday, and Friday only those automobiles with license plate numbers ending with an odd number can be on the road. *On* Tuesday, Thursday, and Saturday, only cars with even-numbered plates *can be driven.*

Copyright © 2003 by Pearson Education, Inc.

41a **Topic sentence, page 129**

4. The American family has undergone significant transformations in the last thirty years.

41b **Supporting sentences, page 130**

Checked sentences: 2, 3, 5, 7, 9, 12

41c **Paragraph unity, page 131**

Crossed-out sentences: Indeed, fossils of ancient corn cobs can be found in museums today.

Today the United States grows about 80% of the world's corn and is the world's largest exporter.

41d **Paragraph coherence, pages 132–133**

1. and
2. In contrast
3. The first
4. for example
5. In other words
6. On the other hand
7. For instance
8. First
9. like
10. Otherwise
11. Because

41e **Concluding sentence, page 134**

2. These three reasons explain why cockroaches will probably exist on this planet long after our own species disappears.

42a **Introduction, page 135**

A.		B.	
a.	2	a.	3
b.	3	b.	1
c.	1	c.	2
d.	6	d.	4
e.	4		
f.	5		

42c **Conclusion, page 136**

2. In conclusion, uniforms offer advantages to schools, to parents, and to students. Schools benefit from improved safety and an atmosphere that promotes learning instead of competition based on clothing. Parents benefit from the reduced cost of uniforms, and students benefit from their convenience. All these factors explain why a majority of people surveyed favor requiring uniforms in their children's schools.

Copyright © 2003 by Pearson Education, Inc.